WELCOME

TO MY

WORLD

WELCOME TO MY WORLD

Johnny Weir

Gallery Books

New York London Toronto Sydney

I dedicate this story to the lovers and iconoclasts
who never stop the world from spinning,
and to the two people who have taught
me the beauty of life and love—
my mother, Patti, and my father, John

 Gallery Books
A Division of Simon & Schuster, Inc.
1230 Avenue of the Americas
New York, NY 10020

First Gallery Books hardcover edition January 2011

GALLERY BOOKS and colophon are trademarks of Simon & Schuster, Inc.

For information about special discounts for bulk purchases, please contact Simon & Schuster Special Sales at 1-866-506-1949 or business@simonandschuster.com.

The Simon & Schuster Speakers Bureau can bring authors to your live event. For more information or to book an event contact the Simon & Schuster Speakers Bureau at 1-866-248-3049 or visit our website at www.simonspeakers.com.

Designed by Jaime Putorti

Manufactured in the United States of America

10 9 8 7 6 5 4 3 2 1

Library of Congress Cataloging-in-Publication Data

Weir, Johnny, 1984–.
    Welcome to my world / Johnny Weir.
        p.   cm.
        1. Weir, Johnny, 1984–. 2. Figure skaters—United States—Biography. I. Title.
GV850.W45 A3 2011
796.91'2092 B—dc22   2010044198

ISBN 978-1-4516-1028-4
ISBN 978-1-4516-1137-3 (ebook)

Contents

Prologue

get more messages than Jesus. Actually, make that Santa.

My BlackBerry and iPhone won't stop their incessant buzzing. First it's my best friend Paris (and no, not the heiress) on the personal line, then a very hot and very young, supposedly straight guy who attended my weekly *Weeds* night fête and complimented my cupcake selection. *What could he want?* Not the time to find out. Ditto for the calls and texts on my professional line: record producer, ice show producer, reality show producer. It'll all have to wait.

Right now the only distraction that matters is the wailing intercom in my manager Tara's Manhattan apartment. Our driver has been angrily trying to get us downstairs and into the car for the last forty-five minutes.

Just a few more seconds for a last look in the mirror. Other than a black Viktor & Rolf jacket over a stunning emerald green chiffon Pucci blouse, the rest of my outfit is pretty much the Johnny Weir uniform: black skinny jeggings and pointy black Christian Louboutins. Joey, my makeup artist, has gone way over the top with my eyes to match the magnitude of tonight's event. A final turn to check out my mullet, newly dyed magenta (an absurd little touch that lands me on both People.com and PerezHilton.com the next day), and we're off.

The Town Car races just a few blocks east through Hell's Kitchen and over to Sixth Avenue, where a mad jumble of photographers and gawkers gather in front of Radio City Music Hall. We could have taken a cab the short distance. But celebrities don't take cabs, Tara says, they take cars.

"I'm not a celebrity," I say to her as the driver opens our door. "Just an ice skater."

Instantly we are enveloped in craziness. On the red carpet of the *Sex and the City 2* movie premiere, where it's names, names, names, I have to keep my jaw from dropping open (I don't want to look bad in photos, after all). Chris Noth walks by, then Donald Trump, quickly followed by *Ugly Betty*'s Becki Newton. All the Gossip Girls bring up the rear.

Anyone who is famous and in New York City is on that carpet.

"Johnny! Johnny!"

My name is being shouted from every angle. Photographers want me to give them flair and TV reporters want the crazy quotes. But even more surreal are the stars trying to get ahold of me. Gabourey Sidibe, an Oscar nominee, stops to tell me she's a fan, right before I get a big hug from the French actor Gilles Marini. I can't believe people whose lives are splashed in the pages of *Us Weekly* or *People* know my name.

I can't even believe I'm *at* this premiere, but I received my invitation from the star of *Sex* herself—my icon Sarah Jessica Parker. Daytime talk-show host Kelly Ripa (who has been a longtime supporter of mine but became an überfan after the 2010 Olympics) and her husband, Mark Consuelos, had me and Tara over to their gorgeous, two-story penthouse for dinner, where we were sipping wine when in walked SJP escorted by Bravo exec and on-air personality Andy Cohen.

I had a mini heart attack deep down inside. A fan of *Sex and the City* since the show started, I have always wanted to be Carrie Bradshaw. The character informed a lot of my youth and fashion daring; she inspired me to be a New York–style single lady.

She held out her hand to me and said, "I'm Sarah Jessica."

"Of course you are," I said, awestruck. "I'm Johnny Weir."

"I know exactly who *you* are," she said with a Bradshaw-esque glimmer in her eye.

Sarah Jessica was everything I imagined she'd be: sweet, tiny, beautiful, good smelling, kind of like a fairy-god celebrity. We all sat around under the stars on Kelly and Mark's roof deck, enjoying delicious food, talking about projects and kids. I felt just like one of the ladies.

Before Sarah Jessica left, we exchanged contact information and she invited me to her big premiere. I was still on cloud nine and already crafting an outfit in my head when an hour and a half later, I received an email from her with the subject line: "This Eve." "Such an honor to meet you," she wrote. "Look forward to seeing you at the premiere."

So tonight, thanks to Sarah Jessica, I'm having a true Cinderella-cum-Carrie-Bradshaw moment. Inside Radio City's theater, there seems to be a star in every other seat. Tara spots Jennifer Love Hewitt wearing the same Hervé Leger dress as she, completely making her night (especially after I tell Tara she wears it best).

As we slowly make our way down the aisle, someone taps me on the back. Turning around, I realize it's Vera Wang. As the famed bridal designer turned designer of everything including mattresses, she is a legend in her time. But she was also part of my competition, having designed the 2010 Winter Olympic costumes for my archrival Evan Lysacek. As if that weren't bad enough, she decided to trot out some nasty comments about *my* Olympic costumes in the press. She tells me she'd been misquoted in the press and wants to bury the hatchet. Vera Wang doesn't have to apologize to me. She's Vera Wang. But I accept.

Glancing to Vera's right, I notice Anna Wintour, a sight that sends my heart into palpitations. To me, Ms. Wintour is everything. Not only is she the ultimate dominatrix of style, but I love how she runs her magazine and how brutal she'll be to get ahead. Even if you don't respect fashion, you have to respect her for being on top of her industry for so long.

Vera must have seen my eyes darting in the *Vogue* editor-in-chief's direction because she decides to introduce us. "This is my friend Anna," she says in the way of only the very rich.

For me, this is on par with meeting Lady Gaga or Christina Aguilera, a big, big moment. I don't know how to make my approach. Usually I like to hug and kiss on both cheeks (I'm like a mobster and hug everyone I meet, even businessmen). But Anna is already sitting in her seat, so I don't want to climb over Vera to hug and kiss her, risking the possibility of my tripping and squashing the tiny fashionista to death and ending her reign at *Vogue*. No, I definitely don't want that to happen.

So I have to settle for extending a very well-manicured hand to take hers. It just doesn't seem proper, though. So while she's holding my hand, I curtsy as if she's the Queen Mother and say, "It truly is an honor." Then I beat a hasty retreat lest I start to stutter like a fool.

As we continue down the aisle, Tara leans in to me and asks, *"Who was that?"*

"Are you fucking kidding me?"

After deciding to never ever speak to Tara again because she doesn't know who Anna Wintour is, I take another look at our tickets. Where are our seats? We are still walking toward the front of the theater, past Anna Wintour and Vera Wang, past Suzanne Somers and Donald Trump. We even pass Liza Minnelli and we're still going. All these bigwigs and legends have worse seats than me? When we find our seats—down front and dead center—I feel absolutely gorgeous and successful. I think to myself, *This is exactly where I like to be.*

The *Sex* premiere comes and goes, swirling among the countless events, meetings, awards, and obligations that make up the whirlwind I call my life. Ever since the Olympics, that spectacularly individual moment on the ice when my fate as an athlete was finally sealed in artistry and controversy, I have done anything and everything under the sun.

Here's an abridged list:

—Went to the Kentucky Derby in a giant black Chanel sun hat decorated with a white rabbit carcass

—Toured the Fashion Institute of Technology to decide whether I should attend design school

—Judged Miss USA Pageant in a multipastel Chris Benz feather coat because I didn't want the beauty queens showing me up

—Hired a stylist

—Accepted an award from GLAAD

—Landed a book deal

—Filmed an episode of *The Rachel Zoe Project*

—Filmed an episode of *The Soup*

—Did a voice-over as a waiter on *American Dad*

—Appeared on *The Wendy Williams Show*

—Held meetings about a fashion line

—Did a photo shoot for MAC Cosmetics

—Skated in a benefit in Harlem hosted by Donald Trump
—Wore headbands to everything
—Taught a skating seminar to children to Indianapolis
—Met Cher after attending her concert
—Commentated on the World Championships for TV
—Got snapped by paparazzi while birthday shopping for my mom with my brother in SoHo
—Recorded a single called "Dirty Love"
—Appeared on *The Joy Behar Show* twice in one week
—Appeared on the *George Lopez* show twice in one week
—Covered Elton John's Oscar party for the E! network
—Met Kelly Osbourne, love of my life
—Took meetings about a perfume and skincare launch
—Appeared as a judge on *RuPaul's Drag Race*

Friends and family think I'm crazy to run myself ragged on the heels of a soul-wrenching, medal-less Olympics. "Take it easy and give yourself some time," they say. But at this point I'll take almost anyone's call, because I have to figure out the next chapter of my life. I want to explore all the opportunities being handed to me because I know they won't last for long.

Plus, quiet reflection and waiting is not my way. For the past thirteen years, it's been beaten into me to never look back.

As a figure skater, sitting in the kiss and cry area—that little box at a competition where we wait alongside our coaches with TV cameras trained closely on our faces for our scores—everything you have worked so hard and so long for comes down to a few numbers. You kill yourself and give everything to be ready for an event, and then in a flash it's over, leaving nothing in its wake but a profound emptiness. Whether you have achieved a medal or failed miserably, loved or hated the process of getting there, in that second you fall to the pit of your existence.

You feel tired. No, you feel dead. And in that state of utter depletion, you have to immediately start building yourself up for whatever's next. The job of a champion is to leave the moment behind as soon as it's happened in order to get back on the ice and start the process all over again.

For so long I stripped my life down to nothing but skating to become one of the best in the world. Despite my many attempts at rebellion, I was constantly ruled by my coaches, training, the United States Figure Skating Association ("the federation"), and other strictures of my sport. And then, in what felt like a heartbeat, it was done.

With all the astonishing adventures and staggering catastrophes of my competitive skating career behind me, I'm in the kiss and cry of my life.

1

A Very Weird Child

Above the bed where I slept as a child, a small hexagonal window let in a vision of the dark woods outside our home. I'd often lie awake at night as the shadows danced across my bedroom wall. The trees would shake back and forth in the wind, a tense crackling noise accompanying their ominous listing. I was sure one of them would crash through the roof, instantaneously and tragically ending my life at the tender age of seven.

My flair for drama, or melodrama anyway, came early.

But as much as I hated that window in the darkness, when the sun shined I loved its view onto the outside world. I was pretty divided about my entire bedroom: a torture chamber by night, my showpiece by day. When my parents built their dream house in Quarryville, Pennsylvania, they involved me in the planning so that I could have exactly the room I wanted. The result included lacy white curtains, a small wooden desk for drawing, and a bright apple-red carpet (my mother, a huge fan of red who even chose it as the color of our kitchen sink, was my inspiration).

I also picked a water bed, just like my parents had. Water beds don't come in kid's sizes, so every night I'd climb into this gigantic bed, my tiny frame rolling on the seductive waves that were beyond my comprehension at the time. Our cat Shadow always slept beside me. I loved that cat, but his incessant kneading filled my mind with visions of the bed popping and drowning us both in a geyser of water. To paraphrase Oscar Wilde, there's heaven and hell in each of us. That described pretty much my whole childhood, including my cat.

The duality was a product of my hyperactive imagination. In the waking hours, it was my biggest asset. A quiet child who loved to play alone, I dreamed up new and fantastic scenarios each day. Sitting in the middle of the forest, mounds of earth became lions in the African veldt and flowers turned into exotic birds. Jumping over fences and tree stumps, I turned into a horse competing dressage at Devon.

But at night my mind turned on me. The hexagonal window was just one example of many, including the horse farm display on the far side of my room. My father had built the wooden stable to house my prized collection of beautiful Breyer horses.

At fifteen dollars a pop, the horses were expensive but I was addicted to them, so every holiday I'd get a new one to add to my pastoral tableau. It wasn't playing I did so much as meticulous art direction. And it got me through the day. Come nightfall, however, the horses betrayed me, their regal faces grimacing like something out of Satan's stable.

Given my troubled relationship with the dark, I needed not one night-light to fall asleep, but three. For good measure, my mom would also put on the radio. She tuned it to a soft rock station, the kind of music she liked to listen to, hoping that the sounds of Eric Clapton and Amy Grant would lull me to sleep.

One particular night, the undertones of '80s synthesizers began to work its calming magic and I felt myself drifting off to sleep. But when the song ended, a commercial came on the air. I don't know what it was for—car insurance, Mothers Against Drunk Driving—but the most terrifying noise of shattering glass and crunching bone filled my room. I lunged for the radio to make it stop and began searching for another station with less drama.

Scanning the dial, I moved past late-night preachers talking about what Jesus wants and classic rock with its whining guitars until something totally unexpected and foreign rose up from the speaker: notes on a piano, then a flute in the background. The ethereal sound, although heavy and somber, made me feel very light. Blue skies and plains with long, green grass broke through the gloom of my room. The music transported me to another world of my own design by giving me the space to make up my own stories.

At the end of the song, I leaned in close to learn from the announcer that the piece was from Chopin and the station classical. A vast and magical world opened up where I could imagine whatever I wanted. I kept the dial glued to the classical station from then on, unaware of the very real places music would one day take me.

———

The truth is, you had to have an active imagination to not go crazy where I grew up. A speck on the map in the middle of rural Pennsylvania, Quarryville's most exotic feature is its Amish people. The isolated subdivision where we lived sat in the middle of seven Amish farms. Kids could walk down the street late at night by themselves, and people put away the locks for their doors long ago.

Town itself consisted of one gas station and one traffic light. An Amish store called Goods sold socks and camouflage gear for hunting, a popular pastime in the area. There was one video store, a Chinese takeout place, and an ice cream stand that only stayed open in the summer. The most extraordinary thing that happened during my childhood was a hot air balloon crashing down in a nearby cul-de-sac. When its shaken riders knocked on our door to ask for help I thought I would die from excitement.

My parents, John and Patti, moved the family to Quarryville

from nearby Oxford, where they had gown up. They've known each other since kindergarten. Dad, a football player, and Mom, a cheerleader, began dating after high school, married, had me four years later and my brother, Boz, four years after that. Jobs at a nuclear power plant in Peach Bottom brought them to Quarryville. For as long as I can remember, they both rose at dawn each day to go to the plant, where my mother had a desk job and my father was an engineer, and returned at night for a family dinner.

Despite the fact that my parents led conventional lives and didn't stray far from their roots, they had an energy that compelled them to do things their own way. Especially Mom. While everyone in her family made chicken and dumplings by rolling out the dough into flat noodles, she made little balls. But her independence went well beyond dumplings. She's someone who says whatever's on her mind to anyone, including me. When I was a little kid people often mistook me for a girl because I liked to wear my hair long. But if anyone ever suggested I cut it, my mom always had the same reply, "If that's how Johnny likes his hair, that's all that matters."

She likes nice things, too, and taught me about taste. Walking into a store, she'd turn to me and say, "Okay, Johnny, I'm telling you, I'm going to pick out the most expensive thing here. And then we're going to have to downsize and pick something different." And we always did.

Many nights I'd watch from the edge of her bathtub as my mom got ready to go out to a party. She'd spritz herself with

Estée Lauder's Youth Dew (a scent that she started wearing religiously at the age of thirteen and is indelibly marked on my olfactory memory) and brush back her short, dark brown hair. Her wide-set eyes, high forehead, and square chin, which she had inherited from her father, were almost an exact replica of my own.

I'd play with the lipsticks and eye shadow until she left the bathroom to pick out an outfit, then watch as she perused her vast leggings collection (it was the '80s after all) for a pair to wear that night. A tiny woman, five foot three and very thin, my mother loved fashion. She had polka-dotted dresses, leggings in every color under the sun, and a lot of hot heels. She was crazy, crazy, crazy for shoes.

While my dad slapped on his Old Spice, she settled on a pair of black leggings, pink pumps and an oversized cream top with shoulder pads. I thought her outfit was so glamorous. "Yes, Mommy, that looks good," I said, offering my unsolicited stamp of approval.

I liked that my mom was different from the other moms. Her short, slick hair was a far cry from the long, flowing bouffant that was the 'do du jour back then. She had a rebellious streak and didn't care what anyone thought about her.

My dad shared my mother's independent spirit, but in a quieter way. A strong guy with a big, thick neck, my father built tree houses and forts, whatever my brother and I asked for. As a kid, I thought my father was fearless. Once he decided to burn a huge pile of leaves he had raked in the yard. But he put a little bit too much gasoline on it, so when he threw the match on the pile, flames shot up and his arm caught on fire. Wearing only a T-shirt, he scooped up my brother and me in the nonburning arm and ran away from the leaping flames. After throwing us into the neighbor's yard, he rolled to the ground and put himself out.

My dad's toughness extended to his parenting style. When he gave my brother and me chores, they had to be done perfectly. After I weeded the flower bed and in between the brick walkway, he would inspect and, sure enough, finding a few tiny, missed seedlings, make me do it again. And again. And again. He wouldn't tolerate anything half-finished. I hated him for his meticulousness when I was little, but now I get it. As much as my mother gave me my free spirit and love of special things, my dad taught me to balance that with an appreciation for discipline. You need to get everything done and done the right way before you can enjoy yourself.

Mom taught me about style, Dad about effort. What they gave me together was respect—for other people, but also for myself. My parents never made me feel odd, even though I definitely didn't act like all the other kids. When I spent hours lining up my toy animals in neat rows only to put them away again, they applauded my power of concentration. My mom didn't mind when I played with her shoes, and my dad got me riding lessons simply because I asked him. That's why I believed in myself a lot.

While most kids get awkward if their friends make fun of them for something, I never changed my behavior because of what anyone else thought. Even as a seven-year-old boy, proudly showing off my new bike with streamers on the handlebars (my mom had bought it for me; Dad was against it) I didn't let the other boys' taunts ruin my ride.

"That's for girls," they all laughed.

"Well, *I* like it," I said.

Heckling only eggs me on, making me want to become more of whatever it is that people are mocking. So the next day I returned to the boys' hangout, riding my new bike, only this time I had braided the streamers to make them even prissier. So what if what I liked didn't match up with that of others? Life was whatever I wanted to make of it or make it into.

The boys didn't respond and left me alone from then on. I wasn't always right in my choices—maybe the streamers were a bit silly—but I needed to figure that out on my own terms.

2

The Natural

As a child, my mercurial imagination was matched only by my boundless energy. I hated to sleep when I thought about all the activities I could be doing. During the day, I ran the soles of my sneakers down from my various obsessions: track, roller skating, gymnastics, anything that wasn't a team sport (which I despised because I'm simply not a team player, and never will be).

My parents did their best to accommodate my every interest. During my gymnastics craze, my father built me a set of balance beams in the backyard where I practiced the dips, turns, and hops I'd seen on TV, not allowing myself to progress to the next level of beams until I had fully mastered the moves on the shorter one without falling. I pursued all my hobbies with the zeal and seriousness of a pro, even if I had no real idea what I was doing. When I got to the highest beam, I completed my routine by jumping off, then raising my arms in an Olympic salute, thousands of adoring fans in my head cheering for me.

So it was that my parents ended up buying me a pair of beat-up black leather skates from Play It Again Sports, our local used sporting goods store, after the images of Kristi Yamaguchi winning gold for her country in the 1992 Winter Olympics in Albertville, France, sparked my fancy.

My family always got Olympic fever during the winter games. It must be the Norwegian blood from my dad's side coursing through us like an icy bobsled track. We knew the names of all the top athletes, their hometowns, even the cheesy made-for-TV backstories. My dad loved the skiers and bobsledders, but for my mom and me it was all about the skating. That year Kristi was a revelation, all steely confidence and extravagant costumes.

With Kristi in mind, I laced up my new used skates, the blades as dull as butter knives, and flung open the big French doors that led onto the deck and out to the cornfields behind our house in Quarryville. The cold air blasted me full force. I had never been so happy to feel ice and wind in my life. The area had been hit by a blizzard and for the last five days my mother, father, brother, and I had been trapped inside with six-foot-tall snowdrifts blocking the doors and windows. It's a miracle my brother and I didn't kill each other—or that my parents didn't kill the both of us.

The sun was out and shining over the vast white landscape. My destination was in sight: a snow-cleared patch of ice in the middle of the cornfield. I took off, running down the stairs in my skates, through the yard and out to the field. The cold filled my lungs and the sun warmed my cheeks as I sped across the yard. All that was missing was the theme song to *Chariots of Fire*. But then out of nowhere I caught a blade on a frozen tree root and went flying face-first into a snow bank. Not exactly an Olympic moment.

But eventually I reached the ice. Although it was my first time on ice skates, I'd logged considerable hours on roller skates in our home's sprawling unfinished basement. The gray cement was the perfect surface for figure eights to various classical music cassettes my parents bought me for holiday gifts, and I used the steel support pole in the center of the room to practice turns.

I was pretty sure these moves would translate to my rock-covered ice patch in the middle of a cornfield. In my mind's eye, I was gliding smoothly and effortlessly in a sleek sparkling costume, the crowd of adoring fans chanting my name. Of course, anyone who saw me that day must have wondered who the crazy kid was in the beat-up blades, hopping over small stones and pumping his arms like he'd just landed a triple axel.

---

definitely caught the skating bug that winter afternoon in the cornfields. The feeling of speeding from one place to another so quickly was amazing. And that might have been the start of my career on ice if not for a certain dapple gray Arabian horse-cross Shetland pony named Shadow (no relation to my cat). My parents had bought him for me after my love of equestrianism grew way past the meticulous Breyer display on my bedroom shelf and into a serious commitment to competitive horseback riding. I'd been around horses since I was a baby, but shortly after turning nine, something inside of me clicked—probably the fact that my dad had competed in horse shows as a kid and had a small chest filled with pretty ribbons to prove it. I told him I wanted to learn to ride the way he had.

I started taking lessons in English saddle and fell in love instantly. I've always been intensely competitive—if another kid could climb up a tree in two minutes, I wanted to be able to do it in one—so with the framework of instruction to channel my innate ability to focus, success came quickly. When my trainer Sue said, "You have to work on your posture," I went home and sat perfectly straight for two hours until my back was shaking. In school, when all the other kids were sleeping on their desks during a moment of quiet, I practiced making my ankles stronger by lifting and lowering my feet for a beautiful line in stirrups.

I won my very first show and within a year was close to making the national team, despite the fact that I was young—and small for my age. It was clear I had a future in horseback riding, so much so that my parents uprooted the entire family from our dream home when I was ten so that I could be closer to my training facilities. The old leather skates wouldn't be making the journey.

As much as I appreciated my family's sacrifice, I wasn't thrilled to be the newest resident of Little Britain. Quarryville hadn't exactly been a thriving metropolis, but compared to Little Britain it felt like Paris in the springtime. The exotic Amish had been supplanted by lonely and desolate land.

I was on the horse seven hours a week, but that still left plenty of time to kill. My parents, perhaps worried that I might find devil's play to pass the time, continued to look for activities to occupy me. Nearly two years had passed since my foray in the cornfields, but I still talked about ice skating, and I still busted out the roller skates every chance I got. And so, Christmas morning in 1994, several months after we moved to Little Britain, found me unwrapping my first pair of real figure skates—black beauties with blades so sharp they could cut skin. And that wasn't all. The gift also came with a package of group lessons at the University of Delaware's professional skating rink, about a forty-five-minute drive from our new home.

The ice rink was littered with kids flailing around on skates. My group name, the Orange Triangles, said it all. I'd signed on for lessons to jump and spin like the beautiful skaters I had seen on TV, not trudge around the ice being called by the shape of a construction sign.

The shapes were a necessity. They were the only way the teachers could keep track of the hordes of kids on the ice during lesson time. Blue Circles, Green Squares, and Orange Triangles separated fifteen different groups of at least twelve kids. It was a veritable Grand Central Station on ice. At eleven, I was the oldest kid by far in my group and the only boy to wear figure skates. The other lads in their hockey skates gave me a few weird looks but I had absolutely no interest in being a hockey brute.

The hour-long lesson almost over, I couldn't wait for the hour of free skating that came in the package price. The teacher had spent most of her time on falling and getting up on the ice (the first thing anyone learns in figure skating). Decked out in my favorite black tracksuit made out of windbreaker material with big green and purple triangles on the shoulders, I was ready to let it rip. The University of Delaware Ice Arena, as big as a small stadium, fueled my imagination.

So did Oksana Baiul, whom I had been transfixed by while watching the 1994 winter Olympics (the first to be played separate from the summer games). Along with the rest of the universe, my family had been glued to the TV watching to see if Nancy Kerrigan, the favored American, would take home gold. But my heart belonged to Oksana. She was *so* much more fun to watch. Her skinny body, adorned in a pink costume with marabou trim on the sleeves, moved fluidly and musically. She was exotic, from a far-off land called Ukraine, which I'd proceeded to do book reports on (I loved to trace the Cyrillic alphabet from a book I found about the Soviet states, imagining myself wrapped in fur and riding a large sleigh through a mysterious and snow-swept city). When she won the Olympics, I wasn't surprised. And the uproar after—that she didn't deserve it and the competition had been fixed—made me love her even more.

As soon as I was released from the gulag of my group, I took off. No longer a novice with two lessons under my belt, I was a champion skater like Oksana with imaginary fans who began to fill the seats of the arena. But to be a real skater, you had to jump. Any idiot knew that. So that's what I had planned for today—to do a jump like I had seen on TV.

I didn't know it at the time, but I had been unconsciously training myself to be a figure skater. Through the movement of roller skating and the rigor of horseback riding, I was very aware of my body and its different functions. On a trampoline in back of our house, I had spent the summer practicing rotating like the skaters on TV, jumping up, spinning, and landing.

I headed for a small opening in between a girl tottering in bright pink pants and two boys pushing each other hockey style. Once in the clear I pushed off on one leg and jumped forward, flying in the air as I rotated around one and a half times, and landing backward. It felt just as great as I had imagined, and I planned to spend the next fifty-two minutes doing them again and again while my adoring fans cheered me on.

But my group teacher interrupted me.

"Johnny, do you have any idea what you just did?" she said, pulling me aside.

I had no idea she had been watching me. ·

"Yeah, I jumped."

"You did an axel. That usually takes someone at least two years to learn. You just did it in two hours."

———————

I wasn't too sure about this lady. Priscilla Hill, my new skating teacher, showed up to our first lesson wearing a snowsuit . . . in the summertime. It wasn't even a cute girl's snowsuit but rather a big puffy gray one from the U.S. Air Force, for which her husband flew planes. She also called me Johnny, which I hated. Although my family called me that to differentiate me from my dad, at school and in my professional life I went by John. I tried correcting her a bunch of times, but she seemed not to take notice. Very happy and smiling all the time, Priscilla had an extremely childlike aspect that made me feel like she was younger than me. Her accessory of choice was a backpack in the shape of a panda bear.

The teacher who had noted my axel brought me to Priscilla not only because she had won national medals during her competitive skating career and now coached a lot of good skaters but also because she was a "lefty" like me. Those who rotate counterclockwise when they skate only account for about 20 percent of people, and it's important to have a coach not confused by the difference.

After one lesson, Priscilla gave me her opinion: I had a lot of talent but I needed more time on the ice. A lot more time. At eleven years old, I was practically middle-aged for a figure skater. My skills weren't nearly up to par, she said. Just as you have to practice a foreign language, I would have to work every day to become fluent. Once a week certainly wasn't going to cut it. We needed to move to Delaware because Priscilla didn't want to work with me after "he's been in the car for a long commute and exhausted," she told my mom and me.

Move to Delaware? I was floored. We had just moved for my horseback riding, plus I didn't want to live in a totally different state, away from all my family and friends. From the minute the first teacher pulled me from the crowd, I knew I wanted to be in the Olympics. But I didn't realize everything that it entailed. I didn't realize that I wouldn't be able to live a normal life or keep riding.

I definitely didn't understand the financial strain of paying for all my activities. I had a good riding pony, which costs the same as a car and is expensive to maintain. Now my parents were faced with paying for a skating coach and renting time on the ice.

My mom, however, understood I couldn't continue to ride horses and skate at equally intense levels. The money issue aside, I wouldn't have been able to keep both up, plus go to school. The next day she sat me down at the breakfast bar facing our kitchen and said, "Johnny, you have to make a choice. Are you going to ride or are you going to skate? Because we can't afford for you to do both, and your body can't handle doing all this stuff."

It was such a big decision, one that would affect not only my future but that of our entire family. We would have to move again if I chose skating, and to a totally different kind of environment. But my mom was content to leave it up to me. Even when we were little, she respected her kids and let us make up our minds about pretty much everything.

She left me at home to "sit and figure out what you're going to do" while she went to the grocery store. For the next three hours I stayed glued to my stool, staring at the white tiles with blue flowers of the bar and contemplating what would be the right choice for my life. I kept alternating between the image of myself as an Olympian in horseback riding versus figure skating.

My mom finally returned and, after putting the groceries away, asked if I wanted a sandwich. "Please," I said. She made me my favorite—roast beef with tomatoes—and sat down next to me. "Okay, Johnny. You've been alone long enough; did you make a decision?" I immediately started crying because I had made a decision, and it was a hard one: "I'm going to skate."

"Are you sure?" my mom asked because she'd say "Are you sure?" about everything. "Are you sure, Johnny?"

We were both crying by this point.

"Yes, Mom. I'm going to be a skater."

In the spring of 1996, after only about ten months of living in Little Britain, my family packed up again to move to Delaware. Other than the trauma of my having to say good-bye to my pony Shadow, none of us shed too many tears about leaving the house in the middle of nowhere.

My extended family, however, was pretty shocked and upset. A number of them came down hard on my parents about moving not once but twice for the fancy dreams of a kid who hadn't even hit puberty. "What the hell are you thinking?" one aunt said. "Why are you leaving Pennsylvania, everything you know, and your big beautiful house to move to a shit box in Delaware? It's a cesspool down there."

But my parents didn't listen to any of it. As kids, both of them had a lot of dreams smashed before they could even start—whether because of strict parents, too many kids in the house and not enough money, or simple small-mindedness. They never wanted to regret having said no, so they did everything within their power to help me achieve whatever fantastical notion I set for myself.

I had to agree with my extended family on one point: our new house was kind of a shit box. At least compared to what we were used to back home. No more rolling hills, cornfields, forests, or quiet cul-de-sacs. Now we looked right into our neighbors' windows and it really creeped me out. I kept my blinds shut tightly at all times; I've always put a high premium on privacy.

Luckily, there wasn't too much time to dwell on Delaware and its shortcomings because I got swept up immediately in the ice rink. During that first summer program, I spent almost all day at the arena, five days a week, without ever stepping outside, even though the arena wasn't more than eight minutes from our house by car.

My parents and I got up at four o'clock in the morning, early enough for them to drop me off and get to work at the power plant in Pennsylvania on time. By five o'clock I was out on the ice training with Priscilla. Because she didn't want me to acquire bad habits, I wasn't allowed to skate without her supervision. So by seven o'clock I was off the ice with about ten hours to kill before I could get back on the ice at five for one last hour of practice.

The rink—where I ate my packed lunch from home at a makeshift table using one of the chairs from an administrator's office and took naps on a stretching mat in an open area above the stands—became my babysitter.

Because Priscilla had decided I would do pairs skating, as well as skate on my own, I had to do weight training in order to become strong enough to lift my partner. The trainer at the rink had his work cut out for him: I was a tiny, skinny kid for the longest time. At four foot nine and seventy pounds, people used to ask my mom all the time if she was feeding me.

I was fine with the weight training, but I really hated the dance classes that were also part of the summer program. There were five different teachers, one for every day of the week, including the un-jazziest jazz teacher on Mondays and a fat lady who taught modern dance Thursdays, and I despised all of them for boring me—except for Yuri on Wednesdays.

Originally from Saint Petersburg, Yuri Sergeev had danced with the Kirov Ballet and had a strange accent not unlike my idol Oksana. While he taught us Russian, Greek, and Moldovan folk dances, I had the same thrill as when I used to trace the Cyrillic alphabet from my book on the Soviet Union. Except that Yuri was alive and able to return my excitement.

He took me under his wing, offering me ten extra minutes after class to privately coach how to hold my arms or head in ways that would look good on the ice. I was built in a way that Russians favored when looking for kids to train as skaters, so Yuri knew the best positions for my body, and I loved the extra attention.

For the most part, though, I spent my time watching other kids practice and train. Seeing the skaters at the junior and senior levels go through their programs, get tangled in frustration, and work it out with their coaches was my greatest lesson during that period. I began to differentiate the styles from little clues like a straightened arm or tilt of the head. I was a sponge drinking up anything and everything that would make me a better skater.

The ice rink was a haven where I made friends who were equally passionate about skating and so made me feel comfortable expressing myself through music and movement. It stood in stark contrast to life outside, which was foreign, and not in a good way. Living in a new state, my parents, brother, and I were away from all our friends and family in what seemed like a big city filled with traffic lights, noise, and dirt.

As the temperature outside the rink dipped with the arrival of fall, I faced yet another terrifying aspect of my new life: school. I showed up the first day totally unprepared for the experience of eight hundred kids in an unruly urban middle school. My first mistake was my outfit. A small, pale kid, all eyes and lashes, I had chosen to wear jeans that hit a little above my ankle and a big, brightly colored polo shirt and my backpack with the straps on both shoulders. It's like I wanted to be killed.

I couldn't believe my eyes. Rocking big baggy jeans and ripped apparel were kids, if that's what you could call them, in all colors and sizes. There were Asians and Jews, Muslims in head scarves and lots of African Americans. I had never been so close to black people and now they were knocking into me, big boys with as much facial hair as my dad.

It didn't take long for the other students to find out that I was a skater—I only went to school half days to accommodate my training schedule—and begin calling me a "homo" or "faggot" when I walked down the hallway. They would sing aggressively anti-Johnny raps. But I was always strong enough to take that sort of thing. Especially now that I had skating to wrap myself in: it was my art and nobody could take it from me.

———

"So where did your son skate before this," one of the other mothers asked my mom at the rink.

I was working on my double jumps, rotating twice in the air and coming down with a haughty flourish I'd developed with Yuri. Priscilla was yelling at me to stop jumping around and concentrate on my footwork. All I wanted to do was jump and have the arena whirling around me. I didn't care at all about technique, but Priscilla beat it into me. She discovered my inner talents, the edge quality I became known for, and forced them out.

"This is the first place Johnny's skated at," my mom answered. "He's only been skating for six months."

"No way; he's too good," another mom said. "You have to be lying."

Nobody believed my mother, Priscilla, or me that I had just started because I could already do a lot of the spins and jumps that the older kids were struggling with. I could do them without thinking, while they were falling and falling and falling. On the ice, it was clear that I had something special, but the other parents gossiped that I was keeping a secret. My mom hated it, but I love it when people talk about me.

I never wanted to do something that I was going to be mediocre at, even as a kid. So if I wasn't a star, I would still pretend I was one. But when Priscilla would talk about me ("Oh, I have this wonderful boy I'm training") or I would notice the other coaches coming to watch me while I practiced, I knew it wasn't all in my head.

But I still had to prove myself in competition. My first big trial was the qualifying competition for the Junior National Championships in Pittsburgh. My training up to that point had been fast and furious to the point of dizzying. In order to get to the qualifiers that September, I had less than three months to pass a total of eight tests required by the U.S. Figure Skating Association (USFSA) for competing on an official level. I had already participated in a bunch of small, local competitions to get ready for battle. Although I had always won these contests by a landslide, I didn't know how I would do on a much larger stage.

At my rink and even in the local competitions, I was in a safe nest where I was coddled by all the coaches and the other kids around me. Because I was one of the only boys in my age group, everyone rooted for me to keep pushing. If I learned a new jump or new program, they told me how great it was. But would I skate as well surrounded by an arena full of strangers?

When we all piled into the car to make the drive from Delaware to Pittsburgh, the cool fall air smelled faintly of burning leaves. My skating partner Jodi Rudden and I had worn coordinated orange (me) and red (her) turtlenecks in homage to the season. She and I were similarly opinionated, driven, and outspoken, and we even looked alike with our pale skin, dark hair, and tiny bodies. The matching turtlenecks drove home the effect. In the car with my mom and Jodi's mom, Janice, we were bouncing off the walls. It was the first time that I'd really been away. I couldn't wait to stay in a hotel and eat in restaurants like a real grown-up.

Pulling up to the arena, the number of kids who had come to Pittsburgh to compete was bewildering. The South Atlantic region we were part of extended from Pennsylvania all the way down to Florida. I was up against twenty-two boys in my division of the singles skate, more than double the number of any of my previous competitions. Plus, the South Atlantic region has always been known as the strongest, the hardest, and the most talented group on the East Coast. Scanning the boys in my group, many of whom had the shoulders of miniature linebackers, I suddenly found the prospect of eating at T.G.I. Friday's not all that appealing.

I competed in singles first. The rink was smaller than the University of Delaware's arena, but family and skating fans packed the stands because my group, juvenile boys, were young and cute, a real crowd pleaser. We were divided into groups of six and thanks to the Weir family luck, which is not good, I drew to skate last in the last group. Waiting for boy after boy to complete his program, listening to the thunderous applause or, horror, the gasps of falls, proved utter torture.

By the time my group got on the ice for our six-minute warm-up period, I felt sick to my stomach. Those minutes ticked by as slowly as a century, but when they were over I made a beeline, still wearing my skates, for the lobby. Standing in my costume, I found my mom and said, "I want ice cream."

I don't know if I thought I was on death row ordering my last meal, or if the dairy would soothe my bubbling stomach, but I just needed something to calm me down. My mom rushed and got me a vanilla cone from a nearby stand that wasn't doing too much business. I took a few licks and stoically returned to the rink.

Priscilla, who had traded her snowsuit for a big fur coat in honor of the event, guided me to the ice. I had gone about six shades paler than my already translucent skin. I felt awful. *Why did I want to do this in the first place? I am a horrible person for selling Shadow and now I am going to pay. I'm not ready. What was Priscilla thinking, sending me out after only six months of training?* A piercing shriek from the crowd broke my spiraling thoughts.

"Go, Johnny!"

It was my partner, Jodi. I looked up and saw her in her red turtleneck screaming for me. A whole group of people that I trained with—all the big kids and their parents—surrounded her. They pumped their fists and made catcalls.

Then my music started, and I did the only thing I could do: I went out and skated. After a whirlwind of jumps, spins, and footwork, I had earned all first place scores from the judges. Not too long after, Jodi and I killed in pairs, earning all first place votes, too.

We qualified for the Junior National Championships, which would be even harder than this competition and require a lot of training between then and April to be prepared. But more astounding than qualifying was the realization that, yes, I was as good as everyone said I was. It wasn't all in my head. I floated home on the assumption that my entire future would come just as easily and naturally, but I was in for a rude awakening.

3

A Star Is Born

I sized up the other boys on the ice and thought, *I've got this locked up.* Not knowing what to expect at the Junior National Championships, I initially approached the biggest contest of my life so far with a fair share of trepidation. But during the practice right before the competition, I figured out that no one else could do a triple jump. In the five months since the qualifying championships in Pittsburgh, I had learned *two* different ones and had incorporated both into my program. A boy to my left landed with a thud during a double axel. Oh, yeah, I had this.

So far the trip out to Anaheim, California, had been a fantasy come to life. My partner, Jodi, and I traveled together—we were also competing in the pairs—and because it was spring and the West Coast, we ditched the turtlenecks for matching shirts: purple, the color of royalty. On my first long flight, I played a *Wheel of Fortune* video game my mom had bought me. This was heaven.

Bright, beautiful California felt like a different planet from dour Delaware. The sun shined all the time and people sold tropical fruit on the side of the road. Our hotel was big and comfortable, just how I like them. Young skaters from all over the country filled the elevators, rushed through the lobby, and caught up with old friends in the lounge. Because I was very shy, I didn't make it a point to mix with the rest of the skaters but I shared in the excitement of our common goal.

During the warm-up, I felt extremely confident. But just like in my old bedroom, when my happy impressions would flip once the sun went down, my peace of mind vanished in the moments before the competition. As I waited for the announcer to call my name, my previously positive assessment of my chances of winning turned on its head. Suddenly I became convinced that I *wouldn't* win. This was the first time I was performing the triple jumps in front of people at a competition. The best skaters in the world fell while doing them on TV all the time, and I hadn't even been skating a year yet. Everything that had given me confidence became negative.

I couldn't turn the worrying thoughts off. I knew they were my nerves flaring up and assumed they would sort themselves out once I settled into my program. But they followed me onto the ice and flew alongside me like harpies while I skated. I had grown a couple of inches in the last several months and my long legs suddenly felt as if they belonged to someone else.

The real problem, though, was my head. During my program, I made five or six mistakes and finished up with a curious mix of bewilderment, anger, and fear. However, nothing could prepare me for the shock about to come. When the judges presented their placements, there were all these different numbers I had never seen before: 14, 5, 6, 2, 13. I was used to seeing all ones. "What does this mean?" I asked. Well, what it meant was that I placed fourth in the men's competition when I should have won it and experienced my first major loss. I was shocked. Even though I had been nervous, I hadn't imagined not winning. I'd never truly contemplated failure.

———————

Forget Jodi. Panic was my most trusted companion for the next two years as I went from a kid to an Olympic-level athlete. After my first taste of losing at the National Championships, I discovered another part of myself that couldn't be controlled simply with hard work and talent. I was never sure who would show up on competition day—confident Johnny or the guy who choked. Just like the vivid thoughts in my head as a child that made my environment delightful during the day and conversely paralyzed me at night, the force of my personality worked both for and against me.

Very often I did well. After moving from juvenile up two levels to novice, I won the regional and sectional championships and then placed third in the National Championships in 1998. Right after turning fourteen, I won a Junior Grand Prix event in Slovakia, beating a lot of high-level junior skaters who were older than me.

But just as often, I didn't do well. In 1999, the year I learned to do a triple axel, the jump necessary to compete at the Olympic level, I completely psyched myself out during my first competition of the Junior Grand Prix in the Czech Republic and suffered a humiliating defeat, coming in seventh.

I was all over the place. On the one hand, I decided I wanted to go to the 2002 Olympics in Salt Lake City, Utah. I knew I wouldn't be a champion, but I thought I could make the team after only five years of skating, which was ludicrous. On the other, I was completely out of my comfort zone while competing. It didn't matter that I trained every single day, going through the exact same routine perfectly without problems. As soon as I stepped on the ice for a competition, I started sweating and my heart raced. Every imaginable bad thought worked its way into my head: *you're ugly, you're lazy, you're just not good enough*. I was my harshest critic.

My big problem—one that stayed with me for a long time in my career—was that I didn't know how to compete. Unlike most kids who start on the ice at three years old, getting their makeup done, wearing costumes, and learning to compete against other kids, I went right from zero to national-level competition. I didn't get that comfortable kiddie period to learn how to react in different situations, how to deal with stress, and, most important, how to keep nerves under control. Going from zero to sixty, I was crashing left and right.

I was also becoming a teenager. What a combo. When you're an angst-ridden hormonal mess, that's a *wonderful* time to undergo constant scrutiny.

As I started to grow hair in places where I didn't think people should have hair, I sprang up from my long-standing height of four foot nine to five six while barely tipping the scales at a little over one hundred pounds. I was still a beanpole, but a bigger beanpole. With my body changing, I not only had to deal with normal anxieties but also keep adjusting my techniques.

By the 2000 National Championships, I had a full-on career crisis at the ripe old age of fifteen. Even though I fell on my triple axel in the short program, none of the other skaters tried one, so the judges still put me in first. But then, with the expectation of winning that I found crippling, I had a complete meltdown in the free program. Obsessed with trying not to fall, of course I fell. It was my first competition against Evan Lysacek, a then skinny waif from Illinois. Until my debacle during the free program, Evan had been in fifth place. Ultimately he won and I took fifth.

Everything changed as I climbed the ranks of competitive skating. My body, my technique, my ability, my emotions, my surroundings, all in turmoil and flux. The one constant, however, was that I sucked at competing. People from around the world were saying the same thing: "Johnny's wonderful. He can do triple axels and is great in practice. But in any contest, he falls apart."

Struggling with my mental stability, I asked myself, *Can I do this?*

<hr>

The Chinese skaters, in their government-issued costumes, accepted their scores grimly. This was the last place on earth I wanted to be. I had told the USFSA flat out I didn't want to go to the Chinese Junior Grand Prix, but they sent me anyway. And when the federation says go, you go. They wanted me there because I was the only person from the States at the junior level who could do a triple axel. Like Russia's junior skaters, the Chinese were a group that everyone feared because they could all do really difficult jumps. They were a bitch to contend with.

Seven months after the Nationals, those embarrassing falls still hurt. I hadn't forgotten what a rotten job I had done and still didn't know how to beat down my nerves. And here I was, facing skaters who didn't seem to have any emotions, only perfect technique. I was also a bit wobbly, having subsisted for the prior couple of days on nothing but black coffee and energy bars I had carried with me from home (I don't do Chinese food).

All I had going for me was the fact that this competition didn't really matter. In all the years competing in the Junior Grand Prix circuit, I had never made the finals because of my terrible track record. Winning some competitions and losing others, I never gained enough points to make it all the way and this year was no different.

So I hit the ice without inhibition despite it being the first time I chose to include two triple axels in my long program. No matter how many mistakes I made, Priscilla's philosophy was to make everything harder. Never step back, always step forward, even if it hurts. But the pressure of hard programs never bothered me, only the pressure I put on myself, and that was completely gone in China. I skated perfectly in both programs and took second place to a Chinese boy, which exceeded everyone's expectations, including my own.

My personal victory in China set off a winning streak that restored my confidence and that of those around me—crucial since I was moving to the next and highest group in skating, the senior level. These are the skaters who are on TV and go to the Olympics; these are the ones who really count. Three weeks later, back in the States, I moved from the regional competition to the larger sectional, defeating everyone on the East Coast. People started to whisper about me doing well in the next National Championships, a totally unexpected rumor for a newly minted Olympic-level skater.

I felt a new and odd sensation: calm. Even as the months flashed by quickly and I arrived in Boston for the 2001 National Championships, *the* event that dictated who went to the World Championships and the Junior World Championships (and helped define early favorites for the following year's Olympic team), I remained comfortable in my skating. I didn't know if I was learning or simply getting over a phobia, but I prayed my new Zen state stayed.

I should have been scared. At sixteen, I was the youngest competitor in the senior level by four years. On top of that, the week before I had sustained a bad hip flexor injury, which required a cortisone shot three inches from my naughty bits that left me without much feeling in my hip while I skated. But being the underdog is where I flourished. On top, I needed to worry. I really didn't think I was going to do anything but show up—maybe get tenth place if I was lucky. After my short program, to my astonishment, I placed sixth, which meant I was in the group of skaters who performed their free program live on ABC Sunday afternoon. For the first time, I was going to be on national TV.

When I got on the ice to warm up the next day, I couldn't believe the men skating around me. They were the best six skaters in the country, and I was part of it. Watching the big American champions like Timothy Goebel and Michael Weiss, whom I had followed for years on television, spin and stretch in the flesh didn't feel real. *What am I doing here?* I thought before remembering that I had to stop staring and start practicing.

Before I even touched the ice to compete, I had already won. As part of "the group," the best six, I would get my pick of Grand Prix events that fall and a shot at the 2002 Olympics. After all my personal issues, I was so honored to be there and returned the honor by skating my ass off. The big tassels on my costume's shoulders shook as I shimmied and danced to my raucous Hungarian music. I rocked it so hard and clean. Although I placed last in the group, I couldn't have been happier: sixth in the country was not a bad place to be.

Sofia, Bulgaria, in March is not pretty. I arrived in the Eastern European city as the highest-ranked U.S. skater competing in the Junior World Championships after my performance in Boston. Spring was nowhere to be found among the crumbling smog-stained buildings and empty streets. Even though morning was fully under way when the taxi spewing exhaust picked my mom, Priscilla, and me up from the airport, a gray mist filled the deserted vista. Occasionally a person, bundled head to toe from the cold, popped up looking like a walking cocoon.

The Junior Grand Prix series takes skaters to really obscure places like Banská Bystrica, Slovakia, and Hamar, Norway, because it lacks the funding of the senior series. Although it's a European capital, Sofia came as a shock to our little traveling band. I stared out the window of the taxi, marveling at the desolation. My anxiety mounted as the bleakness extended. I was a pretty finicky traveler who always felt uncomfortable abroad. Just dialing a different area code was enough to freak me out. Surveying the alien landscape, I knew I was going to feel *very* uncomfortable here.

I was jolted out of my reverie by the taxi lurching to a halt in the middle of the street. There wasn't another car or person on the road as far was we could see, so why had the driver stopped all of a sudden? My mom, clearly suspecting a scam, glared at the driver while Priscilla, as she was known to do in any uncomfortable situation, began laughing loudly like an overgrown kid.

"What's going on?" I asked the driver in my faltering Russian.

Because of my interest in Russia, I had taught myself some simple phrases and figured he might understand me since Bulgarian is very close. Unfortunately, I had no idea what he said back to me. My mother was able to surmise his meaning when the driver jammed his finger at the windshield.

"Johnny! Dogs!" she said.

Right outside the cab, a pack of wild dogs snarled at us. The twenty or so mangy, wolflike canines bared their teeth and howled before taking off for a dowdy Soviet-style municipal building. Oh, no, I was definitely not comfortable here.

My surroundings weren't the only reason for my discomfort (although it didn't help when the people at the hotel registration said, "You can turn right out of the hotel during the day, but only right; never go left. And at night, don't leave the hotel at all.") I had trained hard for the event and was skating well, but the pressure was on like never before. Every single person knew who I was.

At the arena the day of the event, one of the USFSA officials came up to me, accompanied by a few of his foreign counterparts. The white-haired official, in a Brooks Brothers blue blazer and khaki pants that made him look like he had just stepped out of a Florida golf club, gave me a big scary smile.

"This is our next great skater," he announced as he patted me hard on the back. "Watch him now. Soon he's going to be our next champion."

He might as well have jabbed a blade into my leg. I entered my short program with the needling sense that I was going to be a big failure. I blindly made my way through a routine, which included a triple axel–triple toe loop combination, the hardest thing that anybody was doing on the ice during the event. But that's not where I fell. It was during my last jump, a triple flip, that I landed on the ground. A jump I had learned three years earlier! Trudging off to the kiss and cry box to await my scores, I was so disappointed. The judges didn't see it that way, though. They kept me in first place, despite my fall, firmly sticking behind their choice for the next generation of Olympic skater. One of the first things you learn as a figure skater is that the judges give special treatment to their favorites. Going into the competition, they always have an idea of who the best skaters are, and that guides them in their scoring.

The weight of number one crushed me as I readied myself to compete in the long program the following day. It was more of an unraveling, really. When I looked in the mirror of my locker room, I saw a fraud. A big, ugly, stupid fraud. With bad hair. In the reflection, the short spikes were clearly crooked. Great, I hadn't even done my hair well.

As the second-to-last skater in the event, I was forced to sit backstage like a caged animal ready for the slaughter. Listening to the raucous audience reactions for the other skaters, like

Evan, who was second to me after the short program, and the scores being read on the loudspeaker as they reverberated through the massive building, I was a dazed and crying mess.

Panicking like never before, I couldn't stop sobbing. Priscilla sat nearby, helplessly silent. While she was a good friend and a great coach, constantly pushing me past my limits and always expecting more, she wasn't good at the raw emotion thing. So I just sat there and wept until she stood and said, "Okay. It's time to go."

I got up and wiped my face. Chin up, jacket slung over my shoulders, I let Priscilla walk me out as the boy before me, who hadn't done very well, finished his program to anemic applause. Junior-level competitions don't draw a big crowd, so the stands were sparsely filled with random, glum-looking Bulgarians and American supporters in their various brightly colored windbreakers.

When I stepped on the ice, the audience began a slow clap that steadily got faster and faster in anticipation of my performance. The increasing tempo made my heart race with terror. Shaking, I couldn't look at the stands for fear that I'd faint and I couldn't look at Priscilla, because I'd start crying again. So I just started skating around in little circles.

I needed some kind of release. There was too much emotion coursing through me. The panic became physical discomfort, an illness corroding an otherwise healthy body. I needed to snap out of it, but I didn't know how.

"Next on the ice, representing the United States: Johnny Weir," the announcer said over the loudspeaker.

Nothing was right. The fans were strangers and the rink decrepit. I hadn't eaten properly in this Eastern Bloc country for an entire week. Everything around me was foreign and uncomfortable.

And then I heard the first few bars of my music, a synthesizer's ominous imitation of balalaika accordion music.

An amazing thing happened: the rink dropped away and the faces receded as "The Heart of Budapest" enveloped me like an old friend. The only thing that I knew in that building at that moment was my music, and I let myself fly upon the normalcy offered up by its folk harmonies. That song and I had spent a lot of time together.

It guided me through my program perfectly. I got off the ice to excited screams from the crowd and hugged Priscilla. After the judges read my scores and named me the new Junior World Champion, I started crying and so did Priscilla. Looking up into the stands, I found my mom and she was tear-streaked, too.

The pain of fear had given way to a burst of accomplishment. The first time in my career that I relied on my muscle memory and let my body do what it was trained to do, the moment marked a huge milestone in my life as an athlete. Music's ability to move me, something that had alleviated my fear of the dark as a child, inspired me to become an artist and then returned to teach me how to become a competitor.

4

Enfant Terrible

Adrenaline coursed through my body as I pushed across the ice. And this was only practice. My first time in Russia—Moscow, no less—marked a homecoming of sorts. Ever since my earliest connections tracing the Cyrillic alphabet and finding a kindred spirit in Yuri the dance teacher at my rink in Delaware, I had continued to develop a love for the country and its dramatic skating style. No matter that my Russia was a mythical one of sable furs, vodka shots, and tsars that had little to do with secret police, bread lines, and bureaucracy. It got to the point where the Russians came to think of me as one of their own, making this a golden place for me to skate.

The pressure was on during my first trip to the real country in the fall of 2002 to compete in the Cup of Russia, the Russian Grand Prix. The judges, officials, and coaches eagerly anticipated my arrival: they had been waiting to see this American who skated like a Russian since I had won the Junior World Championships a year and a half before. "Johnny looks like a Russian on the ice, so we're excited for him to compete," an official told Priscilla and me on our arrival. "He'll be accepted well."

The high expectations of how I would do (something I never felt comfortable absorbing) wasn't the only thing making me nervous. Despite the way I entered the ice like I owned the place, the deep dark truth was I had no idea whether I could get through my whole program. My condition wasn't where it should have been because my training wasn't what it should have been. I just needed some space. Eighteen years old, I was entering my adolescent rebellion on the late side. In truth, I was completely sick of hanging out with Priscilla and my mom.

But this wasn't the time to start doubting myself. I had a big competition tomorrow and right now I was practicing . . . in Moscow . . . for the Russian Grand Prix . . . in my beautiful new costume. I couldn't wait to warm up the sparkly onesie since it was the very first I ever designed. Performing to music from Cirque du Soleil, I had been going for a deranged circus look. The black velvet pants traveled up into a turquoise Lycra top layered with black fishnet (I'm a sucker for netting). To show off my lithe but fully mature body, a turquoise string snaked up my sides and around my waist, ending in a rip at one of the shoulders. I looked like I had just fallen off a trapeze and was very proud of the overall effect.

The American judges walked into the arena and over to my coach while I ran through my program to see what this tight little number could do. I was deep into my impression of a tragic Weimar circus performer when one of the judges ordered me over to him with an angry wave of his hand. As I skated closer, I saw Priscilla's face had gone white and she had the awkward smile she always had when we were in trouble.

"What is *that*?" the judge said as he pointed at my outfit. "This is totally a slap in the face to us."

"He looks like one of them, a Russian!" another judge said. "We can't let him go out there like that."

I couldn't believe what the U.S. skating officials were saying about my perfect costume. Yes, I preferred the more form-fitting, one-piece costumes favored by male Russian skaters to the big pirate blouses and cheap tuxedo pants that the American men wore. But this was a completely original design created by me. They hadn't seen anything like it before.

"You are going to have to change your costume," the first judge ordered.

I started to make my way off the ice as my tears turned the arena into one big blurry white prison. I couldn't simply "change my costume." My costume, like my choice of music, helped create the mood and character of the program. It offered another dimension to consider, aside from landing all the jumps and completing all the spins. In short, it helped me compete.

Much like A-List actresses who won't hit the red carpet unless they're dripping in five million dollars' worth of diamonds, I can't skate unless I feel beautiful. When I perform, my hair and makeup have to be done and I need a costume with a story. That's why I've always had a big say in what I wear on the ice, even when I was younger and wanted things that were unrealistic for my size. Skating to classic Russian balalaika music when I was thirteen, I had demanded a full Cossack costume with big, billowing pants, boots, and a little vest. But because I was so tiny I looked like a child survivor of a pogrom wearing a dead soldier's uniform and had to admit I couldn't really pull it off.

Still, I always had an opinion. When I moved from junior level to senior level skating, Stephanie Handler, my faithful costume designer, put in shoulder pads to chunk me up a little bit because I was a wispy fifteen-year-old kid competing against guys who were in their mid- to late twenties. I freaked out, finding the padding not only cheesy but also distracting since they sort of flew around in the wind when I was skating.

Once I went through my growth spurt around seventeen and got my man body, I was ready to act like a man—and design my own costume. After seeing the Cirque du Soleil show in Philadelphia, I was inspired to sit down and sketch different silhouettes and color schemes. I knew I wanted a Russian-style skating costume: they all wore one-piece catsuits with the whole story of their performance written out on the design. Flamboyant and over the top, Russian men weren't afraid to wear really tight things that showed off their line.

Stephanie said yes to my sexy circus freak immediately. She had been waiting for me to have that moment when I was old and big enough to wear something crazy. My mom and Priscilla approved, knowing that I needed some freedom in my life and preferring it be through costume than other, more destructive venues that tempted me.

When Stephanie finally translated my drawing into the actual costume, I felt a deep thrill wearing it on the ice. I knew I had done something special, something unique.

As it turned out, though—according to the officials from my country telling me I couldn't wear it—the costume was a little *too* unique. Before I could make my dramatic exit off the ice, the first judge caught me by the arm. "One more thing," he said. "Your hair is also disrespectful. Please change it before tomorrow."

I tore out of his grip, out of my costume and skates, and out of the arena. Back in my room, I flopped on my bed, sobbing my eyes out and listening to Christina Aguilera on my earphones. The singer had been the inspiration for my hair, which I had dyed pieces of white blond and fire-engine red, just little pieces. Mostly it was brown. I thought I was making a statement, like Christina, and that it looked good (which, of course, looking back, it did not).

I had been planning on changing it before I went to the

competition, but the geezers from the federation had been so insulting by adding my hair on top of the awful things they said about my costume. Now there was no way I was going to change—my hair, my costume, anything. Maybe they could push me around when I was sixteen but not anymore.

I was ready to leave the quiet Johnny of the Junior World Championships behind and go out on a limb. My new out-there, artistic side clearly came as a shock to some people in skating because they hadn't seen that aspect of me (no one had except my closest friends). But my federation saw my costume, my program, and maybe even me as an affront to American skating tradition.

I was in a jam: if I wore my costume, it would be a big fuck-you to my country. But if I didn't wear it, I wasn't being true to myself. So I did what any self-respecting artist would do—I lied.

I pretended I was sick and withdrew from the competition. I lied to my mother, Priscilla, everyone. Each time a doctor tried to get into my hotel room to check me out, I feigned sleep. I was so terrified—knowing somewhere deep down that my duplicity was costing people a lot of money and possibly also my career if caught—that I practically made myself sick. Despite the fear of lying on all fronts, I couldn't go through with the competition. Who were these people to tell me what to do? No American skater had been accepted in Russia the way I had been and they wanted to ruin it. In the countless hours of hard work I put into creating my costume and program, all they could find was something twisted. Well, I refused to be suppressed.

How did I go from a sweet, skating child to a crazy bitch who tells lies because he can't wear what he wants? My transformation was a gradual one, but my burgeoning divadom had started as soon as I'd returned home from Sofia a year and a half earlier. My ego grew a couple of sizes when I walked into the rink in Delaware to find a huge banner that read "Johnny Weir: Junior World Champion. Congratulations!" and a crowd that began cheering upon my arrival. The skating community crowned me the next big thing, and I was ready for the title. This year Junior World Champion, next the Olympic team. I was finally headed in the right direction. Or so I thought.

The federation treated me like royalty, sending me to the Goodwill Games in Australia in August of 2001, a huge televised event where I competed against the top ten skaters in the world. I was paid ten thousand dollars just to show up—incredible, considering I would have probably shelled out to be in the company of my idols like Irina Slutskaya, Michelle Kwan, Evgeni Plushenko, and Alexei Yagudin. Initially overwhelmed to be part of such an elite group, I skated well enough to earn ninth place and back pats from the rest of the men. I wasn't yet the best, but I belonged.

My becoming a celebrity (at least in the skating world) had the unfortunate timing of coinciding with my late-bloomer's adolescence. Although I was nearly eighteen, I displayed all the signs of rebellion that kids who lead less sheltered lives than a competitive skater go through much earlier. Now that I was a star, I decided I had to dress the part. I tossed the timid polos and practical track pants of my youth, taking my fashion cues from the boy bands popular at the time. *NSYNC had it going on as far as I was concerned. I waltzed into my ice rink in a thin tank top with "Rock Star" blazoned across it in sparkles and my hair colored with various shades of store-bought dye.

I didn't experiment with drugs but rather my identity. My new favorite catchphrase was "Fabulous!" and absolutely everyone in the world became "honey" as I became freer with my personality. Now that I was a grown-up, I wanted to do as I pleased (although looking back, there is nothing more immature than declaring yourself a grown-up, and no life less free than that of a competitive skater). While before it would have been rare for me to stay out past dark, now I began spending a lot of time away from home with friends from the rink. We would watch movies late at night at a friend's house and then head to a diner afterward. When that got boring, we would sit in one of our cars and watch drunk people make fools of themselves outside the 7-Eleven. Either way, I often didn't get home until 2 a.m. But hanging out—that's what adults did! However tame my rebellion sounds, it was pretty unusual behavior for a training athlete.

The only people not giving me the respect I deserved were my mom and Priscilla. They weren't treating me like a man, or a star, but rather like a big baby. Was I eating properly? Did I get enough sleep? Where had I been so late the night before? These were questions for a kid, not a champion skater about to turn eighteen years old.

Yes, I started to enjoy having a drink with friends on occasion and I didn't watch my diet as closely as I should (meaning I ate more than a tomato for dinner). Other American skaters might have been horrified: that wasn't top athlete behavior. But it wasn't like I was skipping practice or anything. I showed up, on time, for every session.

Priscilla and my mom might have been on my ass about my new "bad" attitude, but I wasn't too worried. I had gotten this far without paying too much attention to what other people had to say and I intended to keep it that way. My whole career up until this point had come easy—well, except for competing. So what if I wasn't inspired to work hard? My success would continue to happen, just like it always had.

Like most teens and authority figures, Priscilla and I fought constantly. Our biggest battle was over my doing run-throughs, practicing the program with all the elements from the beginning to the end. She wanted me to do them to prepare mentally and physically for competitions. I felt that doing lots of jumps for stamina and conditioning was plenty. "The Russians don't do run-throughs," I told her with a dismissive wave of my hand. "So I'm not going to do run-throughs, either."

I had dedicated the previous six years of my life to catching up to skaters my own age. Having caught up and passed most of them by, I thought I had earned the right to glide on talent for a little while.

However, figure skating is an unforgiving sport where no one gets a pass for talent alone. After I withdrew from the Grand Prix in Russia in a big-time diva fit over my costume, the USFSA dealt a harsh blow by withdrawing me from my other Grand Prix event in Japan. I wouldn't have enough points to make it to the Grand Prix Final, even if I won the event, the federation reasoned, so they didn't want to waste the money sending me there.

Even though it was of my own doing—I had made an incredibly stupid mistake by lying to get out of the event—I was angry at the world for mistreating me. Everyone was so busy putting me in my place when all I wanted was to be an adult, which I thought meant the freedom to do whatever I wished.

I was still fuming over the federation's decision the following day when I showed up for practice. Priscilla, in her snowsuit, stood with her arms crossed like two fat cigars battling each other. I could tell something was up because she normally greeted me with an overly cheerful hello that irritated the hell out of me.

"What's with you?" I asked, lacing up my skates.

Silence.

"I'm not happy about the Grand Prix thing, either. In fact, I'm sure I'm more upset than you," I said.

"That's not what's bothering me," she said.

"Well, out with it."

"You smoked a cigarette!"

"Who told you that?"

"It's not important who told me."

"Then I'll tell you it's not true."

"Kristi told her mom that you were at a party smoking a cigarette. And Sara told Jeff, who told me yesterday while he was coaching."

"Snitch!"

"So it's true."

I just glared at Priscilla in her stupid snowsuit. God, I hated that thing. It was summer, for heaven's sake.

"You're the only student I have who's going to go someplace, and you don't even care about it," she said. "So I'm going to quit teaching, and you may as well quit skating."

Her version of a scared straight speech needed a lot of work. If she wanted to quit teaching, she should go ahead and be my guest. I would find another coach. I didn't need her or anybody else for that matter.

"Fuck you," I said, and left.

———————

I apologized to Priscilla eventually. My mother made me do it ("Tell her you'll never smoke again and it will be fine," she said) after a long week of not speaking to each other. But I didn't fall in line. I continued to practice as I saw fit, running roughshod over my coach's demands, and having fun with my friends at night.

When I arrived in Dallas in January of 2003 for the National Championships, the cracks in my plan of doing things only my way grew instantaneously from tiny fractures to huge fault lines. Because I had withdrawn from the last couple of competitions, nobody had seen me skate practically all year. My condition remained shrouded in mystery, which allowed the skating world's imagination to fill in the question marks with big expectations. A few of the top skaters had withdrawn from the event because of injuries and people predicted I would do great things. They needed at least one showstopper and I fit the bill.

God, was I in bad shape. I had trained every day but I was nowhere near showstopper condition. At least I looked good, I tried to tell myself. For my short program to the Cirque du Soleil music, I decided to wear the deranged trapeze artist costume the officials had demanded off my back in Russia. "Screw everyone," I said. "I'm going to wear what I want." Priscilla, normally a total conformist, was so terrified of me by this point, she didn't argue.

Waiting to go on the ice, I put all my confidence into that costume, as if it could carry me through the program instead of the other way around. I also put a little in a higher power. And apparently He listened. Through some act of God I skated a perfect short program. A private miracle, unbeknownst to the judges and audience, landed me in second place and a shot at competing in the World Championships. No one was more surprised than me.

But a short program is only two and a half minutes long. A long program is four and a half minutes, and facing those two extra minutes the next day brought me to my knees. It's a long xertion time for skaters in the best condition. My mind ran to lack as it had so many times before. Why hadn't I done my un-throughs? Right before I was set to compete, I faced the leak fact: I wasn't prepared. "I can't do this. I can't do this," I murmured softly to myself.

With every TV camera trained on me, I put myself on the ce and delivered a half-hearted pep talk: *you are going to try.* My music from *Dr. Zhivago* started, and I began skating. But hope idn't last long; ten seconds into the program my blade got stuck a between the wall and the ice while I was doing a simple cross-ver.

I went tumbling onto the ice in a tangle of confusion and mbarrassment. It was so crazy I didn't know what to do with nyself. I got up very quickly, and then, even though I wasn't in-ured, put my hand on my back, pretending that there was omething wrong. Lying seemed to have become my default.

Now what should I do? Out of instinct, I had pretended to e hurt. There was nothing to do but go through with it. I opped my program and skated over to the referee.

"Ugh, I hurt my back so bad," I said.

"Well, can you continue?" the referee asked.

Could I? "Yes, I can continue."

Okay, Johnny. Get your shit together. Let's go.

I started skating again and I could feel my audience, the col-ctive anticipation, as I went up into the air. It's the same sensa-on as when somebody's staring at you from across the room nd you can feel it before you even turn around. When you're on the ice, you feel all of these eyes, and you can feel, through their eyes, their emotions. At that moment, it was pure hope.

I landed the first jump. Excited that I wasn't injured, the audience cheered me on. I did the first jumping pass through their slow, rhythmic claps . . . good. The second jumping pass . . . great. I had another triple axel planned and went into the air. It was huge. I felt this is my shot to really rock. My last thought before I came down was *God's going to help me again.*

Then I came down very hard, literally. On my landing, I popped my kneecap out of place and couldn't get up. Finally, this was no lie. After what seemed like an eternity, I rose from the ice and hobbled over to the boards. "I can't continue," I said, and withdrew from the competition.

People's genuine concern for me after the fall made me feel worse because I knew I had brought this on myself. I had wanted to be treated like an adult, but instead had acted like a child. I had wasted the once-in-a-lifetime opportunities presented me and thrown away what should have been the most important season in my career. Now truly injured, I had no idea what it would take for me to get back on track.

A few minutes after I withdrew from the National Championships, an elderly woman, Helen McLoraine, who helped fund my skating career and had traveled from Colorado to watch me compete, fell while she was getting up to leave the rink. I found out a few days later that my benefactress—the lady who had sent my mother money here and there through the years to help with a costume or some extra for music editing simply because she loved my skating—had passed away in the hospital.

Up until that point, I had been the next golden child of U.S. figure skating, and now it was done after I completely ruined the whole season in which I was supposed to make a name for myself. After the event in Dallas, the federation took me out of Envelope A, which assured the top-tier athletes consideration for international events and a little bit of money for training. I could no longer compete at the biggest senior level events such as the World Championships or in the Grand Prix series. My stupidity and hubris had landed me in skating purgatory, cast out from the mainstream and any kind of official track. I knew I had earned my karma and deserved everything that was happening, but that didn't make it any easier to deal with.

I don't do things halfway. As spectacularly as I had risen up the skating ladder, I fell just as hard and fast. In one quick year, I went from an alternate for the Olympics, Goodwill Games athlete, and the next favorite of U.S. figure skating to a complete and utter write-off.

5

Embracing the Starving Artist

My ankles swelled into a war zone of black, blue, and bloody red from the countless footwork passes I'd run through. My hip flexors were slack with overuse from millions of jumps and difficult spins. Every muscle in my body ached. Even my brain throbbed from an entire day of having directives in Russian hurled at me as rapidly and forcefully as machine-gun fire. In a temporary break from my regular training with Priscilla, I spent the summer of 2003 in a program with one of the world's best Olympic coaches. During the insane, grueling summer camp for skaters, I subsisted on coffee and slept in a stranger's extra bedroom—and I had never felt luckier.

I had been so disheartened by the fiasco at the National Championships in Dallas and my subsequent relegation to a skater's no-man's-land by the USFSA that I briefly considered quitting the sport altogether. I didn't think I had the head for it anymore. Resting on talent alone, I had turned last season (when I should have proved myself Olympic-level material) into a total disaster. The skating world didn't believe I had what it took to be a serious competitor, proving that with my new low ranking.

Their harsh voices berated me in my head until I came to my senses. I had never listened to those people before, so why would I now? I wanted to keep skating. I *needed* to. After all my family had sacrificed, personally and financially, for me to pursue this dream, I couldn't give up after encountering a bump in the road (even if the bump was the size of Mount Everest). Plus, I hated when people told me what to do. If the entire federation signaled that I should quit, then I would do the opposite—even if it killed me.

But if I planned on reviving my career after taking a blowtorch to it, a real change of pace was in order. Last year had been a failed experiment in stretching my wings, but the original impetus hadn't been totally wrong. I did need to be away from Priscilla and my mom so that I could learn how to stand on my own two skates. I needed to be inspired.

That inspiration came in the form of a fur-swathed, Dior-toting Russian woman named Tatiana Tarasova. In the obscure town of Simsbury, Connecticut, the world-famous skating coach and choreographer spent summers training an elite group of athletes including Olympic champions such as Alexei Yagudin and Ilia Kulik and my friend, the skating star Sasha Cohen. After Sasha helped me get a foot in the door, I skated for Tarasova. Her only comment, to my mother, was, "Yes, I will take Johnny." Normally she charged in the double-digit thousands for one program, but Tarasova let me train with her all summer for free since I didn't have a penny to my name. Waiving her fee proved she believed in me and offered encouragement before I took even a single lesson. I had been given a second chance and resolved not to blow it.

At the International Skating Center of Connecticut, we skated for about six hours a day, so much more than I was used to, after which I would fall, practically paralyzed, into the bed in the bedroom I rented from a random woman. No matter how stiff or sore I felt, I hit the ice the next morning with the kind of energy fueled by inspiration. Unlike the University of Delaware's crowded rink, here only five truly great skaters trained together.

In the classic Russian style, Tarasova taught us in groups, as opposed to one-on-one, so that we fought each other to be the best. The dynamic brought out the competitive spark still smoldering from my childhood. I definitely responded to all the skaters trying to one-up each other as we vied for Tarasova's attention. The edge of my footwork got sharper and my jump technique stronger.

Entering the session late one day, she began barking in a choppy, aggressive Russian and finding fault everywhere she looked. Although I was far from fluent, I had taught myself enough Russian that I could communicate and understand when others spoke.

Suddenly Tarasova stopped and clapped her bejeweled hands together.

"*Umnitza,*" she said, which was Russian slang for "perfect boy."

I had just come out of a spin in the new short program Tarasova had created for me and decided to extend my leg with a little more bravado than perhaps was necessary. At first I had no idea she was talking to me.

"You look like a young Baryshnikov," she said, giving me a big smile before launching into a list of a million things I had done wrong.

Attracting Tarasova's attention, I felt very special. And surprised. She had praised me for the kind of thing that Priscilla, trying to follow direct orders from the federation, constantly told me to tone down during my normal training life. Skate more like a man; watch your fingers so that they aren't balletic; not so much movement in your hips, please!

But Tarasova appreciated everything that made me me, including my artistic side. She liked my body, which mimicked those of Russian ballet dancers, and provided choreography that enriched the way I moved on the ice. "*Umnitza,*" she applauded me throughout the summer, nurturing the healthy side of my ego and transforming Simsbury into a special hideaway where nothing was too artistic, nothing too over the top. With Tarasova I found my first opportunity to express myself fully and freely.

Not eager to leave this incubator, I didn't take any breaks from the group's training regimen apart for a necessary one to compete in a little local event back in Delaware. It was July and I had been training with Tarasova for less than a month when Priscilla told me at the last minute that I was expected at the Liberty Open at The Pond Ice Arena in Newark, Delaware. The call instantly dealt my ego, which Tarasova had been vigorously massaging, a brutal blow.

In the skating world, there's an unspoken standard: once you compete in the National Championships on television and fight for a spot on the World Championship team, you don't participate in small, local open events like the one in Newark. Those were the competitions where I blew everyone away at the juvenile level when I was just starting out at twelve years old. My entering the event at The Pond was as if Madonna were to try out for *American Idol.* But when Priscilla asked the federation how I could fix my reputation and get things back on track after last season, they responded firmly that I had to return to square one and prove myself all over again. "We need to make sure he's training," an official had told Priscilla, "and doesn't do anything like he did last year again."

So it was I found myself outside the small rink, steeling myself for a humiliating trial. The worst part was that I didn't even feel prepared for this tiny event. July was extremely early to compete. I had just started working with Tarasova and the new short program she created for me was still in process. Meanwhile, we had been so focused on the new choreography that I hadn't yet started doing run-throughs of the long program that I intended to hold over from the previous season.

With my heavy equipment bag slung over my shoulder, I registered myself at the foldout card table near the entrance and after writing my name, the elderly woman distributing the makeshift badges looked up from my signature with her mouth in a little shocked O.

In the skating world I was famous, for good and for bad. So my appearance turned heads in surprise as people wondered why I was there.

After changing into a simple gray and white costume, still a tight onesie that unabashedly showed off my thin frame but reflected my humble status in its lack of adornment, I waited near the ice. The other low-ranked senior level skaters with no chance at a national title sneaked furtive glances in my direction.

"Well, well, well, Johnny Weir," said a judge in a Team USA windbreaker, hair dyed a slightly bluish tint. "What the hell are you doing here?"

The tips of my ears turned red with shame. I stared straight ahead and muttered, "Skating," thinking about how much my mother hated when my brother and I mumbled as kids.

"Oh, you're going to skate for us today?" another judge said, sipping from a large Dunkin' Donuts coffee that smelled sickeningly of blueberries.

"Yes, ma'am."

"Did you hear? He's training with the great Tarasova. Well, I can't wait to see this. That is, if he can stand on his skates long enough."

The judges cackled mercilessly while I burned with my own thoughts. Before the cruel comments, I had felt deeply embarrassed. Now I choked with rage.

Training with Priscilla had been all about the problems with my skating; ours was a nuts and bolts operation. Whenever I headed out onto the ice during an event, I concentrated on my mistakes, which I knew well from hours of having them pointed out, and implored myself not to make them. Although the stage in Newark was tiny, this was the first time I had competed since the Dallas National Championships, the culmination of every single mistake I had made thus far in my career. My history weighed heavy.

But in this small place and moment, something shifted. After the announcer unceremoniously called my name and I took to the ice, the problem child found himself replaced by another one: *umnitza,* perfect boy. Tarasova's voice played in my head, egging me on to remember the art and beauty and forget the pettiness of scores. The power of an Olympic coach telling me day in and day out how good I was fortified me. *Just go out and skate,* I told myself.

And I did. Cleanly, beautifully, perfectly.

Afterward, I took off my skates, changed into my regular clothes, and left without waiting to see my scores printed on the little pieces of white paper. I didn't need to see the proof: I knew I had won.

In Simsbury the next day, I went right back to work, trying to outjump, spin, and sparkle the other skaters in my group. Tarasova, who blustered into our session just as I was completing a triple axel with joyful exuberance flying out of my overly balletic pinkies, clapped her hands in delight. She never asked me how the competition went or uttered one single word about it. This, another of her lessons, programmed me to know that nothing matters but the moment. Whatever happens at an event, good or bad, dissipates when you train on a clean slate of ice.

I stood on the bed and taped a piece of paper to my bedroom ceiling. Then I lay down to make sure I could see the words when I woke up in the morning and before I went to sleep at night. They read: "Johnny Weir National Champion." Clear as day.

Having returned to Delaware at the end of the summer, I refused to lose the drive or inspiration I had achieved with Tarasova and the other skaters in Simsbury. If I were going to be a national, or even international, champion, I needed to strip my life down to nothing but skating. Back home, however, I was surrounded by temptations that knocked me on my ass last season. Friends beckoned with parties or just one quick cocktail. Fried or sugary food appeared particularly tasty after my long workouts.

So I taped the mantra to my ceiling to keep myself in check. "No, I can't come to the party. I have to go to bed early so I can be the National Champion," I said to friends. I did Priscilla's drills like a good boy and chose black coffee over cheesecake because I was dieting to be the National Champion.

Being dirt poor also helped keep me in line. I had a lot of trouble with money because, well, I didn't have any. The federation had cut off my official funding and anyone who had previously given me money had either died or decided I was washed up. I didn't merit a spot on any of the ice tours, where skaters typically make cash to fund their lives, and couldn't get a job like a normal person because my training occupied all of my days.

I love money and, as my mother taught me, nice things, but through my experience that summer with Tarasova, I got in touch with my inner Russian-ness. And Russians, in general, don't have money. So I was fine with not having it, either. I wore my poverty as a badge of a prideful club. I was a member of a romantic long-suffering sect, the Starving Artist. As part of my destitute chic period, I never dressed up for anything and hardly showered. If my hair was greasy from a workout the day before, I simply put it back in a headband. That's what we artists, concentrating solely on the work before us, did. It was inspiring to feel like you had nothing.

The only time I got really fancy and dressed up was when I had my costumes on to compete. Sparkly, tight, colorful, and expressive, they transformed my drab, unwashed persona like a glorious drag queen who only comes alive to put on a show. For my long program, I had re-created the bland gray and silver two-piece, puff-blouse costume from my *Dr. Zhivago* program last season to look like an icicle. Baby blue Lycra covered in white fishnet, paint, and Swarovski crystals, the result was totally razzle-dazzle, much more Russian, and much more me.

The costume for my new short program showed my sensitive side (the depth behind all that glitter). The choreography Tarasova created to "Valse Triste" by Jean Sibelius, a slow, melodic march, had me tell the story of a man who arrives home from war in a suit he hasn't worn since before he left to fight. Waiting for him in his duffel for over a decade, the suit has been ruined by dirt and shredded by time. My costume reflected that image with jagged rips and tears throughout the cloth, an oversized burnt and floppy rose on the lapel. Sorrow that would read on the ice.

Sectionals was another stop on the Johnny Weir shame tour that year. Competing in regional or sectional events is another one of those things a skater at the level of International Grand Prix events just doesn't do. But I did. Because I didn't finish in the top six in the previous National Championship, I had to requalify. Even though I had taken about ten steps backward, my only choice was to keep moving forward.

On the drive to the event, I popped Christina Aguilera's *Stripped* into the CD player and pumped up the volume to liven up the deadly ride. The lyrics to "Make Over" filled up the inside of Priscilla's massive SUV, providing some necessary color to the gray winter landscape. Christina helped me steel myself. Although I had no money or idea what the future would hold, a terrific group of friends supported me. My mom was still my best friend and even Priscilla and I were getting along better than ever. I had no fear heading into quad jumps or driving to an event where I would be something of a laughingstock, because I was in control of my life.

Still, by the time I arrived at Art Devlin's Olympic Motor Inn, where I was staying in Lake Placid, my relentless spirit had begun to relent, just a little. What started as a tickle in my throat turned into a full-blown cold, a fitting tribute to the dreary iced-over town. I have always felt uneasy in Lake Placid. In close proximity to nothing more than cold, dark mountains and miles of trees and townies, the tiny town is horror-movie material. My motel, little more than polyester bedspreads and ugly carpeting, provided no comfort. This wasn't the official hotel of the sectionals where all the other skaters were staying. No, that was down the street and more than I could afford. I had to settle for serial killer lodging. Wrapping myself up in my own sheet so that I wouldn't have to touch the dubious bedding, I took solace in my thriftiness and hoped this Starving Artist might get at least a few hours of sleep.

Though I felt sick and tired the next day, my confidence going into the event soared off the charts. My costumes were unique and gorgeous; I had a short program created by a world-class choreographer; and I was skinny as a rail. Nobody at this two-bit competition could touch me. A few of my friends had generously driven up to watch me skate, which reminded me that although I felt totally alone at times, I wasn't really.

I skated my short program flawlessly, but during my long program, I fell down on a jump. Unlike in years past, however, I didn't unravel at the first hint of a mistake. Because I was far and away going to win, the fall wouldn't hurt me. I stopped for a second on the ice, caught my breath, skated around in a little circle to gather myself, and then gestured to my friends before finishing. A little impertinent perhaps, but eight hours was a long way to drive to watch me skate.

I won and, more important, earned my place at the National Championships. I still had a lot ahead of me to prove that I could be good again, but for the moment I basked in the relief of accomplishment. I knew it was short-lived since, as I had learned from Tarasova, tomorrow I would be back on the ice starting from zero.

However, my moment of glory was even more short-lived than expected. Right after the competition, while I made my way to the locker room to change, a judge approached me.

"You know you're never going to be able to work yourself back from this," he said.

"Excuse me?" I said, although I had heard him perfectly.

"Johnny, just don't expect anything at Nationals. You shot yourself in the foot last year," he said. "You're looking better, and you can obviously skate well. But all I'm saying is you're not going to get any favors from us."

I waited to see if he was finished and then turned to the locker room without offering a reply. There was nothing I could say to him, at least nothing that wouldn't get me in deeper trouble with the federation.

If he or any of his cronies who didn't believe in me had seen the mantra taped to my ceiling—Johnny Weir National Champion—they would have laughed me out of the arena. But his remarks, instead of eroding my confidence, only stoked the fire in my belly. I *would* be the next national champion, not only to prove something to myself but also to shove it down the throat of anyone who counted me out.

————————

Not a single skater who needed to qualify at the sectional championships had won a national title in nearly a decade, but that's what I set out to do when I arrived in Atlanta for the Nationals in January of 2004. I had a goal, but I wasn't an idiot. It would be a miracle if I could pull it off. A lot of famous people were competing, such as Timothy Goebel and Michael Weiss, two of the big mainstays of figure skating at that time. So I had a long list of fierce challengers and skating favorites, plus a panel of judges who practically hated my guts. A miracle, indeed.

I looked good on the ice during practice—boom, boom, boom, landing every jump—and impressed a few stragglers who had come to watch me, probably by mistake. Any pressure I felt going into the competition came from within since, frankly, nobody else paid me any attention. The press wasn't writing about me, fans weren't clamoring for my autograph, and the officials weren't monitoring my practices. As I said, I was a complete write-off.

Flying under the radar, I entered into the short program by psyching myself up with the idea that I had something special to bring to skating in the States—if I could just keep it together. I was a hybrid of Russian and American skating, two very different schools of thought. With coaches from both countries, I had married the artistic with the athletic, the passion with technique. My costumes were different and so was the way I moved my body. I was an American boy with a Russian soul, and nobody else skated anything like me.

Armed with this knowledge, I did what I had done since Tarasova gave me the program—skate clean and perfect and beautiful. I got off the ice and waited for my scores, not knowing what kind of numbers I would receive. I had skated well, but judging isn't a cut-and-dry operation. A whole mess of things go into deciding what kind of number to put to a performance. Technique is a factor but so are subjective notions of skating as an art and the kind of skater who *should* win. Needless to say, politics plays a huge role. The judges consider who they want to be the face of the sport when making their decisions.

When my scores came up they reflected the federation's ambivalence toward me. My numbers were all over the place. For my artistic score, they ranged from 4.9, which was horrible for a senior level skater, to a stellar 5.8 out of a perfect score of 6.0. Because none of the judges expected me to be prepared or skate well, it was like they didn't know what to do with me when I did. After both the technical and artistic scores were posted, I'd received a majority of the judges' votes for first place.

It was a real shock, not just to me, Priscilla, and my mom, but to everyone at the event. In one short program, I went from outcast to first place. The press needed to rewrite the story lines to include me: the skater who had "imploded" in a "disastrous" last season had turned into a "contender."

Suddenly all the skaters and officials who hadn't given me the time of day only a few hours before were patting me on the back.

"You did so amazing!"

"You're skating like the champion we always knew you'd be."

"What happened?"

Just as I had ignored the mean remarks by the judge at sectionals, so I did the same with the praise. Good, bad, whatever, I wasn't going to listen to it because it was all fake. I had my blinders on and reminded myself that every single one of those backslappers had been equally ready to send me home.

I needed that fire and aggression the next day to get me through the long program, which is hard enough to get through without the pressure of being number one. This time, however, I refused to buckle under my virtuosity. After a year of training my mind to believe I deserved the title of champion and following up with the behavior to prove it, I was ready for a repeat performance. I was strong enough now. I could do it.

Unfortunately, I drew to skate last, a horrible, horrible place for someone with my history of nerves to be in. I didn't know if I'd be able to keep up my tough attitude as one by one, the best American skaters performed before me. Michael Weiss, my fiercest rival at this event, skated second to last. A big hulking and classless idiot with three national titles, two world medals, and two Olympic teams under his wide belt, he was a huge star and everything that the U.S. Figure Skating Association wanted at the helm. I sat huddled in the dressing room, listening to every torturous moment, when the crowd erupted into applause for some fantastic jump he landed cleanly. His scores also came through loud and clear. They were great numbers: 5.7's, 5.8's, and 5.9's. Just great. For him.

I left my bravado in the dressing room when it was time for me to compete. Skating around in a little dazed circle, I had my eyes wide open but couldn't see anything. Priscilla tried to talk to me, but I couldn't hear what she was saying, either. I had come down with hysterical blindness and deafness. I fought to stay calm and got into my starting position.

Which Johnny was it going to be?

Good? Or bad?

I started out feeling shaky and too aware of my body. A loose sequin at my neck scratched and the nail on my left big toe pressed slightly into the skate. My breath caught in my chest, flittering about like a caged bird. Then I started to pick up speed in my program. The sound of shearing ice and the visual whirl of the arena drowned out the small discomforts my nerves had produced. The speed, music, and flow combined to give me that rush of great skating. Suddenly I was flying and before I hit the last forty seconds of the program, the crowd had started clapping and hollering.

When I finished, the entire audience leaped to its feet. I couldn't even hear the announcer say, "And again, ladies and gentlemen, Johnny Weir," because people were screaming so much. Everyone was excited over this comeback, me included. A year before I had been lying in the center of the ice with television cameras broadcasting my fraudulent, injured self to countries across the globe. Now I stood in the center, healthy and whole. I didn't care what place I was going to get; this was my victory.

Even though I was clearly the emotional favorite of the audience, sitting in the kiss and cry area waiting for my scores I didn't think I actually had a chance at winning the title. The judge at sectionals had put it plainly: "We aren't going to do anything for you, Johnny." I had said I wanted to win, but the truth was I felt happy to the point of tears at the prospect of earning my first senior national silver or bronze medal.

My technical scores came up, and they were all 5.9's, and 5.8's, higher than Michael's. My pulse raced. Then the second round of scores for artistic merit came up, and I had a perfect 6, 5.9's and one 5.7. All but two judges gave me first place. Now I was really crying. I had won my first national title just as I'd promised myself and everyone else I would.

When you go on the ice to do anything, you're totally alone. You can have the best, most expensive coaches in the world and an entire team of people behind you, but once you're actually out there, it's you that has to do it. I had done everything myself, and I did it my own way.

6

Razzle-Dazzle

I hadn't felt anything even close to love at first sight since watching Richard Gere in *Pretty Woman* at the tender age of six. That's when I first realized there was something different about me. Seeing Julia Roberts get swept off her feet by her rich and handsome client, I wanted to be her so badly because *he* did something so special to me. Kissing seemed like a weird thing to do, but I knew if I were going to do it, it would be with Richard Gere.

As a small child without many inhibitions, I immediately quizzed my friends about the movie. Had they seen it? Did they want to be Julia Roberts like I did? All I got were a lot of funny looks. Nobody understood where I was coming from—especially the boys. "That's just weird," one of them said.

At that age, you have no idea what gay or straight is or any of the ramifications of being different. By puberty, however, I started to get a clearer picture. I came to understand what gay meant, and that many people didn't like it. I also knew that sexually I was gay. But I didn't worry about it much. Perhaps realizing the core truth so young made it easier to accept as I went along in life.

I also didn't feel the need to make my sexuality much of an issue, since at thirteen, I was nowhere close to having any kind of physical contact with anyone, other than hugging my best girlfriends. I didn't wrestle with being gay or let it change my life in the slightest; it simply became a fact of nature, albeit a private one.

Being a serious ice skater was a big part of the reason my "way of life" didn't trouble me too much. I had a job and objective upon which no entanglements could infringe. When you are that young and driven, life isn't a series of random occurrences. Rather, it is a single track shooting toward one thing, and for me that was the Olympics. I didn't bother talking to my friends or family about my feelings, not because I was ashamed, but because it wasn't important to me. Skating was the only thing that had any meaning. And I talked about that *all* the time.

When I did think about sex, which (and this will probably shock a lot of people) wasn't that often, my ideas were very much formed by *Pretty Woman,* hold the prostitution. I have been a romantic forever and even as a young teenage boy knew I wanted sex to be special. I didn't want to be one of these people you read about in sex ed, getting disgusting-looking diseases from casual encounters. I wanted to wait to be in love to have sex. I figured I would be old, say seventeen or eighteen, by the time I gave it up and by then life would sort itself out.

It took me a long time to actually feel really physical. Sure, there were those late nights when, staying up to watch *Oz*, I would feel a strange stirring. But in general, I didn't have any interest in fulfilling my sexual urges. I was way too busy.

Then I had my first kiss with a boy.

I was sixteen at the time, and he was twenty-one—really, there was nothing boyish about him. A pairs skater I knew from the rink, he was very tall and strong, manly aspects I found sexually attractive. But the thought of the two of us hadn't crossed my mind because I didn't scope out guys, plus he was dating a girl at the time.

Late one night he IM'd me and the chat went in a surprising direction.

"Have you ever kissed a boy?" he wrote.

"No, I don't know if I'll have time to," I responded.

My flirting style needed a little work.

"Maybe it's time that you did. I'm having a party. Come and practice."

I got all dolled up for the party, which was filled with older kids from the rink. It wasn't my first drinking party, but I was feeling it. In the few parties I had attended in the past, I would walk in and watch the other kids, guzzling beers or wine coolers in various corners of a house, slowly getting trashed as if I were a chaperone noting everyone's bad behavior. I wasn't a tattle, but I've always felt much older than my peers. Tonight, however, what would normally have seemed stupid to me became exciting.

At six feet tall, my friend usually towered over me, but that night he leaned down close to my face so that I could smell from his hot breath that he'd been drinking.

"It's time to practice," he said, pulling me into a dark corner.

In the darkness of some den, he put his big hands on my narrow hips.

"This is just so I can teach you how to kiss," he said.

Whatever. I was kissing someone for real and it was sexual, dirty and naughty and French. I loved every second of our twenty minutes in heaven. It totally and unexpectedly lit me up.

It might sound naive, but I was surprised by how much I liked exploring the sexual side of myself. With my complete focus narrowly trained on skating, I hadn't given myself much latitude to daydream, let alone experiment with the real thing. Now I had a man, with hair on his chest, no less, who wanted to "practice" with me on a regular basis.

Even though our situation was far from romantic, the pairs skater became my first real crush. The guy was so at war with himself that he would barely talk to me or even look me in the eye, unless it was "practice time." But I was always up for practice.

About once a week he would pick me up at my house under the ruse that we were going to the movies. Instead, we would just make out in his car. Then he would disguise the whole event to himself so he didn't have to face facts. I knew our relationship didn't have a future, but I enjoyed the make-out sessions. I had no trouble divorcing the sexual from the emotional because I wasn't looking for this guy to validate my existence. I was so overly confident in my future: that I would be a champion, make money, be a success. I didn't care what anyone else thought of me. If I had discovered I wasn't too busy for kissing, I was still too busy for a boyfriend, or a girlfriend, for that matter.

After I turned eighteen years old and had officially become an adult, I decided to tell my mother about these feelings. It just seemed like the adult thing to do and I'd vowed that I would be an open and honest adult with the people who mattered to me.

I waited until late one night after my dad had already gone to sleep (my dad is a cool guy but homosexuality is completely foreign to him and not something I was ready to throw in his face). My mom had fallen asleep, curled up on the couch with the cats, while watching *Law & Order*. I shook her awake and looked her in the eyes.

"Mom, I have been eighteen for a week. Adult to adult, I need to tell you something. I'm gay."

Although I knew full well that she had nosed around the rink for years, trying to find out the very information I was telling her, she still seemed shocked to hear it. She couldn't speak and her shoulders went way up around her ears. Suddenly it felt like I was sitting in the room with a stranger, and this was my mom, my best friend. The energy around us dropped as she started to cry.

I wasn't angry. In fact, I had a *Freaky Friday* moment with my mom where I was suddenly filled with maternal impulses. No mother wants to hear her son say he's gay, no matter how wonderful his life is and how well he treats her. Those two little words rip the picture of a daughter-in-law and grandchildren into a million little pieces. I felt sorry for my mom and wanted her to know everything was going to be all right.

But of course, my mom, the superhero, didn't give up her role just because I'm gay.

"I don't really care, Johnny, as long as I know that you are going to be happy," she said. "I want you to be healthy and I want you to have someone in your life."

My mother's reaction, rare coming from a parent, showed me something I already knew: she loves me unconditionally. It doesn't matter what I do; she would never love me more or less. While I continued to maintain that being gay was such a small part of me, it was still a part. So I was greatly relieved that my mother accepted it, because she is one of the few people whose opinion of me truly matters.

Suddenly I felt this great freedom to be out there now that my mom knew I was gay (she was the only person I have ever come out to officially in my family. It's not an issue for the rest of them and they don't ask any questions, which I consider a blessing). For my entire life up until that point, my best friends were all women. But now that I could flounce around and have limp wrists if I wanted to, I began to make friends with a few other gay guys whom I met through skating.

It wasn't easy for me. I am a solitary person who does well in family units and small groups of people. In large groups, like at parties, I shut down and get extremely bashful and cold. The problem is that in general I don't trust anyone, but especially not strangers. As a kid I always thought someone was going to try to kidnap me. As an adult I always think someone is trying to use me.

I definitely didn't trust Paris when I first encountered him. In fact, we hated each other for a long time. Paris was a recent implant to the University of Delaware training facility and to the university itself. Aside from skating, I felt like I had nothing in common with this creature from the dirty South. On the ice, we would exchange nasty looks—two bitchy queens locking crowns.

So when one of my girlfriends invited Paris to the movies with us, I was deeply offended. Not only was he my workplace nemesis (even though I didn't know him), but as den mother of our group, I was the one who made our plans and extended invitations.

After the movies, we were all hanging out, and Paris sat down next to me to make small talk. His rapprochement went off awkwardly at first—he loved Madonna, while I loved Christina Aguilera—but we eventually found common ground in an unlikely subject: the Hilton sisters. Yes, we bonded over Paris and Nicky Hilton. We both thought they were incredibly tacky yet oddly enthralling. He and I fell deep into a discussion of entitlement and the existential meaning of being famous for absolutely nothing. That kind of conversation was totally refreshing. When you come from a small place, a lot of people don't have big dreams or aspirations (like when I'd mention a Birkin bag, not a lot of people got it). But Paris got it, and by the end of the evening nicknames had solidified our friendship: he became Paris, as he was the fun, sociable one, and I became Nicky, the subtle fashionista.

We never called each other by our real names again (Paris's nickname took so well that when the paparazzi shoot him, he's labeled "Paris" in the photo). In Paris, I found a kindred spirit, someone cold, rude, and abrupt on the outside but soft and shy on the inside. After our second time hanging out, Paris was family. In college, away from home for the first time and running all over the place and partying, he needed taking care of, and I love going into that mother hen role. Beyond our love of the Hiltons, that's how we jelled: I found fun in his world and he found stability in mine.

Paris fit into the worldview I had developed in my short and inexperienced life that the physical and emotional were completely separate realms—at least for me. Paris became my closest confidant and constant companion but I wasn't in the least attracted to him. When I came out to my mom, I told her I might still marry a woman. I wasn't talking about sex. Forever and ever and happily ever after doesn't necessarily pertain to sex. I have loved so many women in the way that every husband should love his wife. And you can have sex with a total stranger. I just didn't know if I would ever find sex and love in one person.

Then, a month into working with Tatiana Tarasova in my attempt to undo the mistakes I had made the previous season, I met Alex at a small party after the Liberty competition in Delaware. He was gorgeous—a pairs skater (yes, another one) with clear blue eyes—but I didn't go right to sex in my mind. I'm not an overly sexual person and the possibility of it is never my main attraction. Instead, I was drawn to his mysterious combination of contradicting qualities. He was at once warm and a concrete wall. He gave me his entire life story, but it didn't include the fact that he was gay—which of course he was. He was forthright but uncomfortable with himself. I became immediately infatuated with this sweet, awkward, and fashionably unfashionable boy.

Unfortunately as a skater trying to claw my way back to the Olympic level, I could only pursue one thing at that point: skating. We texted each other a lot of innocuous messages the first twenty-four hours after meeting, but the flame quickly died out. He lived in New England, and I was way too young and naive to know the meaning of long distance.

Still, when Alex sent me a text that he was going to be at the Eastern sectionals in Lake Placid where I was competing to qualify for the Nationals, those small characters, which appeared on my phone, lit my heart on fire.

After the event, I got dolled up in my room at Art Devlin's

Olympic Motor Inn and picked my way through the quiet, dark streets covered in snow and ice to the official hotel where a couple of skaters were hosting a party in their room. At the sectionals, the room parties were way more exciting than the actual competition. Skaters packed themselves into one room like sardines and filled the bathtubs with liquor and ice. This was their well-earned time to get loose. I had gotten all decked because I knew Alex would be one of the warm bodies there.

Outside the hotel room, I could hear the muffled but distinctive sound of drunken voices. When I opened the door, the muted fun turned into the kind of full-on din that normally had me turning on my heels and heading for my pajamas. But tonight adrenaline, some left over from winning the sectionals and more in anticipation of seeing Alex, coursed violently through me in an Incredible Hulk moment.

Almost as soon as I set foot in the room, Alex appeared right in front of my face. His eyes were bluer than I remembered and staring directly into mine with a level of anticipation that matched my own. I had turned this moment over and over in my mind, but now that we were here, I froze. How should I greet him? Alex and I hadn't touched each other before. I couldn't shake his hand—that would be ridiculous. But was a hug too much? I remained frozen, caught between a hug and a shake.

Alex moved in and relieved me of the tension with a big hug. It seemed that someone had become more comfortable with his sexuality in the past few months. When he came in close, I could smell a special mixture of vodka and Gucci's Envy cologne. Why not? Having won his competition, he had his own celebrating to do. Or perhaps he was looking for a little liquid courage.

We sat down with the rest of his friends, but pretty much all my attention went to Alex and reading the signals coming from him. He sat so close to me that our thighs pressed together—*that had to be a sign, right?* Then there was the faux drunken move where he went kind of boneless and draped himself near me.

The greatest sign, though, appeared to me when Alex went up to get another drink. There was something different about him, which I couldn't pinpoint at first. Then I realized: his clothes! When we first met in Delaware I teased him (kind of how the boy in elementary school pulls the hair of the girl he likes) because none of his clothes fit. All of it was in Extra Boy size, that horrible boxy look usually favored by straights. In Lake Placid, my heart leaped when I saw his fitted pants contoured his legs and his shirt didn't blouse out: he hadn't forgotten me and I didn't forget him.

When he returned, I gave him a few signals of my own.

"Come with me," he said.

Alex led me out of the bustle of the party and into another hotel room, this one quiet and dark. The boldness of this previously shy boy surprised me. But as soon as we got inside, his confidence seemed to disappear into the darkness. Our first moment of true physical connection was clumsy and tense in the way of most meaningful encounters where both parties want so much for everything to go right. The pressure of hoping this might turn into something added weight to every part of my body. When we kissed, I felt the vaguely familiar physical warmth from previous explorations, but layered below was a tenderness that squeezed my heart so hard I thought it would pop. The physical and emotional parts of me collided for the first time.

I've never been a good whistler, but after I deposited Alex back at the party and said my good nights to the rest of the crowd (with exultant winks from friends and dirty looks from a few jealous types), I whistled and pranced all the way down the icy path to my room.

I wasn't sure it was possible, but Johnny Weir could in fact fall in love. All it took was a kiss for me to fall for Alex—the kind of descent where your blood sugar dips to the bottom and you get overly excited for no reason. Nineteen years old, skating phenomenally again, and setting my sights on the national title, I felt like I was on top of the world. Adding love to the list gave me confidence on steroids.

For the first time in my life I was tingling from the tips of my fingers to my toes. Puppy love. Lust. True romance. I wasn't sure of the label but I did know this is what these things are supposed to feel like. This is what everyone sings about in pop songs or writes about in books.

We talked almost every night on the phone, but my training made the time in between our visits unbearably long. By the time Paris and I made our first of many visits to New England,

Alex and I were bursting with pent-up energy. We lasted about ten minutes hanging out with the crowd at a skating party before I found myself in a dark room, alone with my very first heartthrob. On a stranger's bed, we made out and played Twenty Questions the way teenagers do.

"We are obviously really into each other, but I want to know what your thoughts are," I said.

"I want to be happy and I don't want you to hurt me," Alex responded.

In figure skating there were a lot of rumors about me—stuff like I had wild threesomes with judges and skaters—all of which were completely false. The skating world is a catty place filled with backstabbing, but because I had been a bitch to so many people during my diva period, it was easy for them to make up stories about me. I wanted to put Alex at ease but didn't know if I could.

"I want to tell you that the majority of rumors about me are false. But if you have a question, you should just ask me directly and I will tell you exactly what went down. I'm not ashamed or afraid and promise to tell you the truth."

"I don't really have many questions," Alex said shyly.

"I want to tell you something anyway," I said.

"What?"

"I'm a virgin."

"Me, too."

"And I really like you."

"I really like you, too."

Revealing deep secrets to each other in the dark, Alex and I both knew whatever we had started that night after sectionals *was* special. We had found love.

As our relationship quickly turned into a committed one, I discovered the unbelievable power in having someone (other than your mother) supporting and loving you in all moments. I also discovered the prickly underside of that bond: other people's envy.

Figure skating, where jealousy runs as rampant as rhinestones, is a fucked-up place to find your romantic future. Still, most of us seek it there, believing that no one else but another skater can understand us. Who else but another skater wouldn't laugh at the fact that I had to go to bed every night at nine in the year leading up to the Nationals? On my first real date with Alex, I ate only a tomato at dinner. A civilian probably would have dialed an anorexia hotline on the spot, but he didn't even blink because he understood that is what you do to get in fighting shape.

It is a human thing to want to bond with someone who understands you, but skating is a small world, making the pool of available love-interests unfairly small to choose from. It's harder to find a decent guy in the skating scene than it is to get into Harvard. Competition gets fierce, to put it mildly.

When Alex and I hooked up, he hadn't really been out. So this sweet and kind kid with clear blue eyes and a very wealthy family represented an untapped and enticing resource in this world of boys who wanted to bang like bunnies. A few skaters in his area pined hard-core over Alex.

Having a bad reputation at the time, I seemed like an easy

target for sabotage. Once we went exclusive, the rumors about my so-called slutty behavior ramped up. However, nobody knew (other than Paris, Alex, and a few others) how big a prude I was in reality. So when one guy with a crush on Alex forced his way into a bathroom while I was using the facilities during a party so he could put the moves on me, he was surprised that I pushed him so hard he knocked his head against the wall. He had hoped to run directly to Alex with news that we had made out. But I don't like shifty games or people barging into the bathroom.

None of that silly stuff ever posed a threat to Alex and me. Raised by two parents who truly love each other, I knew a relationship wasn't a game where you played a part to win the other over. All that mattered was our connection, deepened by expressing our true feelings, no matter what they were. With the strength of that example at home, I was fearless when it came to telling and showing Alex how much I loved him. For Alex, whose parents went from having a home and three kids to going through an ugly divorce, loving someone presented a more terrifying challenge, like bungee jumping off the Grand Canyon.

But together we took the leap of saying I love you and eventually losing the Big V together. Although I had wanted to wait until I was in love, my virginity had never been much of an issue for me. So when I finally had sex, I was surprised at how fulfilled I felt. Staring at each other with smiles from ear to ear, I remember thinking, no matter what, we would always be a part of each other's lives because of this moment.

Of course, a lot of that had to do with the fact that both of us waited for the right person with whom to share that intimate experience.

It is not often that people wait for quality. It makes no difference that I like to have sex with men; my value system is very old-fashioned. I believe there is nothing sexier than knowing one's self-worth. As eccentric and flamboyant as I appeared, I waited until I was almost twenty to lose my virginity, because I wanted it to mean something. I wanted to be in love. I inherited that belief from my mother, who taught me to never settle for less than the best. And in my book, Alex was hands down the best.

While out-of-control has never been my preferred state, I felt crazy alive—"crazy" being the operative word. I would burst out hysterically crying for no apparent reason because I was deeply, madly, passionately in love. That kind of strong emotion made me at once insane and content. It was all brand-new and confusing as hell.

Add to that the new and euphoric peak I reached in my skating career after my win at the Nationals, and honestly I don't think there has ever been another time in my life when I was happier.

Right after I won the title in Atlanta, Alex visited me in my hotel room.

"A lot of people are going to propose marriage to me, so you'll have to stay on your toes," I teased him.

A few days after the biggest skating moment in my life, Alex sent a whole cheesecake to my house with a card that read, "I'm staying on my toes . . . and making sure you eat."

7

Almost Famous

P hotos of famous people from around the world covered the tasteful gray walls of the media consultant's sleek Upper East Side office where I sat waiting. Most of them were signed with little notes, like "You're the best" and "I couldn't have done it without you," to this woman my skating federation had charged with reining in me and my big mouth.

After winning the National Championships, I was immediately thrust into the spotlight with every major press outlet wanting to interview the new, and very surprising, top U.S. skater. But in the very first moment of my media blitz, I got in trouble. During the press conference after the competition, a reporter asked me about my "unusual" free skate costume. Inspired by *Dr. Zhivago,* my gorgeous blue and silver sparkly onesie, snowy and icy in a modern way, required a description to do it justice.

"It's like an icicle on coke," I said.

The statement just came out naturally, inspired by the muse. The astonished reporters looked at me as if *I* were on coke and tried to make sense of a skater who said more than just "I'm so happy to have won." I *was* so happy to have won the event, so much so that I didn't think about the import of my words. But the truth is I never do. Whether it's in a public forum or in my bedroom with friends, I never filter myself.

Almost as soon as it came out of my mouth, the comment was everywhere: television, newspapers, and the Internet, in America and abroad. Drugs! It really freaked everyone out. The big impact of my tiny comment and the number of people I offended startled me. Only on day one of my newfound stardom, I wasn't used to anyone paying too much attention to what I said. My then agent lamely tried to backtrack by saying that what I really meant was that my costume looked like Coke flowing down the side of a frosty can. Did he really think people were that stupid?

Well, I sure didn't and quickly vowed to keep my foot-in-mouth disorder, a Weir family trait, no matter how famous I got. There's always going to be someone who has an issue with something you've said no matter how fake you try to be, so what's the point in bottling up your feelings and thoughts?

Having separate public and private personas was way too complicated for my taste.

The USFSA begged to differ. Livid that their national champion was talking about drugs (plus a few little comments about how bad they were at their jobs), they signed me up for media training the day before I was scheduled to appear on the *Today* show. Everyone worried about how ridiculous I'd be, given the massive exposure on morning television. And I'm not saying they weren't right to worry.

When the woman, a small New York City successful type in a pencil skirt and heels who clearly came from the Barbara Walters school of hair and makeup, introduced herself I knew instantly this was not my people. Sitting behind an enormous desk covered in awards, she threw me a toothy smile that cracked the foundation around her eyes and mouth. Everything about this lady was studied, from her framed credentials to her French manicure. I was so agitated I left my sunglasses on: I had my first World Championships in a few weeks and would have much preferred spending this time training rather than getting spokesperson tips.

"As an athlete, you need to appear centered and focused," she said.

"Why?"

"You're a role model now to lots of younger kids. You have to maintain that image."

This was going to be a long three hours. Instead, I wished she would give me tricks for getting dewy-looking skin on television.

"Can't a role model be funny and clever?" I asked.

"Sure," she said, perking up. "Humor's a terrific way to break the ice on TV. Try a joke, but stick to sports. Only sports. Like, 'I almost put on the wrong skates before I got on the ice.'"

"I don't get it."

The next morning when I arrived on the *Today* show set, I had just enough information from media training to make me very uptight but not enough to be charming. In the car at 4:30 a.m. on the way to midtown, I came down with a case of the jitters. It's rare that figure skaters get the chance to talk in front of the entire country—apart from small sound bites. This was an opportunity for me to present myself through words.

I was also nervous because I had to skate on Rockefeller Center's really small outdoor rink—during a torrential downpour. The last thing I wanted to do was fall on my ass in front of millions of TV viewers. I couldn't wear my costume, which really upset me, because it was too cold and I might get sick. So there I was, in decidedly boring white track pants and a warm-up jacket, with no one to cheer for me around the rink because of the freezing rain. But as they say, the show must go on, so I skated in two inches of rain and by some miracle landed all my jumps.

By the time I finished, I was soaked to the bone but tried to smile for the cameras as rain dripped from my hair and nose. What a TV debut. But the *Today* show anchors were so impressed that I'd skated through the rain without slamming into Rockefeller Center that they invited me to sit on the couch instead of doing my interview rinkside (a coup that maybe also had to do with them not wanting to get wet). I behaved myself like a national champion—well, almost. When Matt Lauer asked me how I was preparing for the upcoming World Championships, I gave a nod to my media trainer. "I'm trying to stay centered," I said. "And not let *Today* show interviews make me jaded."

Today was just the first stop on my new life as a real international skating star. A few weeks later at the World Championships in Germany, I proved my win at the Nationals was no fluke. After flawless short and free skate programs, both of which earned me standing ovations, I finished in fifth place overall. Losing to the Russian firecracker and my skating hero Evgeni Plushenko, the event champion, and beating Michael Weiss, I was thrilled by how the competition went. Tatiana Tarasova, with whom I planned to create new world-class programs for the upcoming season, had worked it for me before my arrival, raving to all the Russian officials about how great I was. Each member of the Russian team, normally standoffish to foreigners, shook my hand, patted me on the back, and said, "Good job." I felt like part of the gang.

Immediately after the competition, I was on a plane with the biggest names in skating, including Plushenko, Irina Slutskaya, Elena Sokolova, and Sasha Cohen, to start rehearsals for the

Champions on Ice tour. Landing a spot on one of the two major ice skating tours in America meant I would be making a steady, and good, income for the first time in my life. In addition to its financial advantages, the tour built up its skaters' egos by touting them as the best and brightest stars (or, in my case, the sparkliest). Touring with Champions on Ice was something every skater, seasoned or not, dreamed of getting to do. From March to May, we toured the country, where every night I soaked up the enthusiastic reception from fans who came to watch me, the country's new champion, skate.

As one of the top six skaters in the world, I was given three Grand Prix events when the assignments came out in June. My first time back on the senior Grand Prix since I had withdrawn in shame three years before, I returned in high style. I was selected to compete in Nagoya, Japan, at the NHK Trophy, in Paris at the Trophée Eric Bompard, and in Moscow's Cup of Russia. All three potentially meant great prize money and more opportunities to make a name for myself. Three top competitions within the span of five weeks presented a heady world tour, but I was ready.

What I wasn't prepared for was the crowd waiting for me when I stepped off the plane in Japan that October. After a twenty-four-hour journey from Philadelphia to Nagoya, I looked more like cargo than human in sweatpants, a loose T-shirt, rumpled cardigan, and baseball cap hiding the hair matted to my head. My skin had the sheen of the great unwashed. So I was shocked and horrified when a group of twenty young Japanese women began snapping my picture after I walked through the sliding glass doors of customs. Luckily I had the presence of mind to wear sunglasses, but I made a permanent note to self to bring a change of clothes, hair product, and makeup on the plane so I'd be camera ready forever after.

At first I was more confused than surprised: why were these people here? Then I saw the handmade signs plastered with hearts, Hello Kitty stickers, and my name. They were here for me. These were *my* fans.

Figure skating fans are a very unique breed of people. These are the folks who watch skating every time it's on TV and not just during the Olympics. They fill the seats of touring ice shows and comment online about every aspect of the sport. They feel like they are part of skaters' lives.

My fans—a core group of ladies called Johnny's Angels (they voted on the name themselves)—are überfans who always go above and beyond. What makes them particularly incredible is that I don't make it easy to be a fan of me. I wear outlandish outfits and say even more outlandish things. Like everyone else in my life, they need to have a thick skin.

Still, if anyone wrongs me, there'll be a battle. And I love my fans for that. Their emotional support is a huge part of my success—so is their financial support. I literally wouldn't be able to afford to skate if I didn't have fans: they have paid for costumes and on occasion coaching bills. That's why I never feel like I give my fans enough, although I work very hard to keep them happy.

Apart from those throwing flowers or holding signs for me at competitions, the airport in Japan was my first time coming face-to-face with regular individuals who loved and supported me—from across the world, no less.

I stopped to sign autographs and take pictures. In return, the fans offered me beautifully wrapped presents of handmade soaps, a fur collar, and anime notebooks—all things they knew I would like from reading interviews with me in the press. One girl had made me a special cell-phone holder covered with rhinestones and little Chanel logos (I told any reporter who would print it how much I loved Chanel, even though I couldn't afford the real thing at the time). I was so touched by the thought and effort.

"How did you know what plane I was on?" I asked her.

"Competition in four days. We wait at airport for two days already," she said.

For me? I was stunned. My own mother wouldn't wait half an hour for me in the car.

"Where Johnny luggage?" another girl said, pointing to the one little bag I held.

"Oh, the airline can't find it. Not even my skates," I said.

The women gasped, a few putting their hands to their mouths in polite horror.

"Don't worry!" I said, trying to put out the alarm. "It should come in a few days . . . I'm in very good shape . . . not a problem if I miss one or two practices . . . I will be fine."

I waved good-bye to them merrily and hopped onto the bus that took me and my mom to our hotel. But that wasn't the last I heard from my fans in Japan. The next day they were waiting for me in the lobby of my hotel (the official hotel of the Grand Prix was posted on the Internet) with bags of socks, underwear, T-shirts, toothpaste, and anything else someone who lost his luggage might need.

I thanked all of them for the thoughtful and helpful gesture. Amid the group of bowing women, I saw the fan who had made me the bedazzled cell-phone cover. She and I bowed a couple of times before she approached me.

"Johnny, it would be my honor to give you special gift," she said.

"You've already given me more than enough," I said, starting to feel a little worried.

"No, please," she said, guiding me to a small seating area off the lobby.

I wasn't sure what was happening but reasoned that she probably wouldn't come on to me, or chop me into little pieces, in front of the hotel staff. What happened next astonished me more than if she had actually wielded a machete.

She handed me a beautifully wrapped box that I tentatively opened, upset about messing up the perfect paper, ribbon, and paper flower. I fished around the tissue for a second before I hit upon something cool and delicate. I pulled out the breathtaking object as if it had just been born. It was a gold and blue enamel Fabergé egg. As she had explained in her faltering English, she had flown to Moscow to purchase one in an authentic shop after reading about my love of Fabergé eggs in a magazine article. I did love the precious eggs but never imagined I'd actually own one. Not even counting the travel expenses, the gift must have cost her a small fortune. And in exchange for that treasure, she asked nothing in exchange except my happiness.

Being a "celebrity," albeit in a very specific world, was pretty wonderful. It was a bit strange to have my photo taken by strangers while walking out of the hotel or buying my fourth Starbucks coffee of the day, but I wasn't complaining. I enjoyed being adored.

The love fest continued when I arrived at the competition and went through the process of accreditation. The Japanese skating officials in charge greeted me warmly and said that coaches in their country were teaching young kids to skate like me—the biggest compliment I could imagine receiving. My porcelain skin and big eyes appealed to Japanese tastes for sure. But the way I skated—into myself and quiet—also resonated with their culture. The realization of my popularity in the country gave me quite a boost going into the event.

When I got on the ice for my long program, a new one created by Tarasova to "Otoñal" by Raul Di Blasio, it was so quiet you could have heard a program rustling. I had already skated well with my new short program to "Rondo Capriccioso" by Camille Saint-Saëns for the pleased and respectful audience. But by the time I had finished the free skate, people were standing and screaming. I even saw women crying. In a country that prides itself on being calm and quiet, the audiences usually barely clap. So this kind of raucous appreciation at the end of the program, very rare for Japan, marked a tremendous debut.

My scores were announced, and I was far and away the winner, beating the runner-up, Timothy Goebel, by more than twenty points. That night, exhausted and elated in my hotel bed, I called Alex to say good night (or maybe it was good morning for him). "It's starting to happen," I said. "I can't believe this. Everything's coming together."

That was pretty much the extent of my celebration, since a few days later I arrived in Paris, where I had to forget the gold medal I had just won and start training for the next Grand Prix a week later.

I'd been to France but always to compete in little towns. Paris was completely new to me and, living in Delaware, a complete treat that I planned to enjoy. Every day after practice I walked the crooked streets, enjoying the intoxicating aroma of buttery croissants and fluffy baguettes (that stuff didn't exactly fit into my skating diet) and lots of luscious dark coffee.

But far and away my favorite cultural delight in Paris was the fashion. Beautiful clothes have always been something I adored and followed like a moth to a flame. But I previously had to relegate my passion to reading fashion magazines since I wasn't able to afford anything much nicer than a pair of designer jeans. But since the Champions on Ice Tour, I had been saving my pennies for this very moment—a shopping trip in the fashion mecca that is Paris.

I walked down the Champs-Élysées and skipped on the Rue Saint-Honoré. It was everything I had imagined. Each boutique window screamed beauty and luxury with clothes by Gaultier,

Lacroix, Galliano, Christian Dior, Chanel, and Hermès. Inside the hushed stores, I joined the ranks of chic ladies in fur-trimmed tweed coats with delicate "CC" buttons and men in slick suits that screamed European glamour. I'll never forget my first big purchase: a pair of caramel-colored Yves Saint Laurent ankle boots with little heels, aptly called the "Jonny." I never dreamed my feet could look so beautiful and almost danced back out onto the street where the scent of cigarette smoke, Chanel No. 5, garlic, and apple napoleon mingled in the air with the angst-ridden soundtrack provided by a lonely violinist and decrepit accordion player. As a fashion addict on his first binge, it was the most erotic time of my life.

I returned to my hotel room laden down with those crisp, life-affirming shopping bags from the world's most beautiful stores, ready to put everything away properly and perhaps try on a few incredible pieces again. Opening the door, I discovered to my abject horror that someone, who had strewn his clothes all over the small room, was showering in the bathroom. It wasn't an intruder but simply another skater. In my mind, the two were equally upsetting.

By this point, I understood some things about myself. Number one: I didn't eat in the cafeteria the organizing committee created for these events, preferring to venture out to the cafés or restaurants of the host city, because everyone would stare at me while I consumed lunch. And number two: I didn't have roommates. These competitions are expensive for federations, so they require skaters to bunk together in order to save costs. But one thing I can't abide is sleeping in the same room as somebody else, especially a stranger. I need my space, and when I'm competing, I definitely need my space.

After enough whining to my reluctant federation (and enough medals around my neck), they let me buy out the other half of the room when I traveled the circuit. It wasn't like I was asking them to pay for it. I had enough extra money to make myself comfortable. I knew other skaters would be jealous and call me a diva, but I didn't really care what they thought. I wanted to get a good night's sleep and win.

Although I had paid to have the small, spartan room with two single beds pushed together to myself, the federation had booked somebody else in there while I was out. My luggage barely fit in there (I do not travel lightly). So I started collecting the stranger's underwear, socks, T-shirts, and pants and stuffing them back into his duffel bag until he emerged from the shower with a towel around his waist.

"I'm really sorry," I said, folding his things a little more neatly. "But I've paid for this room myself. You can't stay here."

"Johnny, when they put me in this room, I knew I shouldn't be here. But there's no other place for me to go. I just had to get a shower and need a little sleep."

"You had your shower, but you can't sleep here. I've packed your luggage again. Please get out."

The poor guy, a pairs skater from Connecticut, threw on jeans and a shirt and fled the room, still soaking, to avoid the effects of my full-on tantrum.

Having a diva fit wasn't my finest moment, but if my federation wanted me to be a star, they would have to start treating me like one. Or at least giving me a room to myself when I had paid for it. The federation found the pairs skater another home, and I held up my end of the bargain, winning the gold a few days later at the French Grand Prix, much to the chagrin of local fans who whistled (the French form of booing) at my victory over their champion Brian Joubert. Beating the world silver medalist from the year before in his own country signaled my ascendancy on the international stage.

Having conquered Paris, it was directly on to Russia. The only problem: I still didn't have my tourist visa to get into the country.

Priscilla and my mom, who traveled with me wherever I went, had dutifully gone to the Russian consulate the day after we arrived in Paris with my official letter stating that I was set to skate in the Russian Grand Prix two weeks later. Because Russians are big figure skating fans, a lot of the people that worked in the consulate knew who I was. It seemed like we would have the visa well before the typical weeklong waiting period.

But we quickly found ourselves caught up in red tape. Every day my mother, who didn't speak a syllable of French, took the Paris metro to the Russian consulate, where she would line up at eight o'clock in the morning and wait for hours until they told her the visa still wasn't ready. We steadily got more nervous until the situation turned into full-on panic when I still didn't have a visa the day before I was supposed to leave for Moscow.

Priscilla, my mom, and I heard rumors the Russians were engaged in a game of payback for what happened to Evgeni Plushenko at the World Championships, held in Washington, D.C., two years earlier. The Americans had held up his visa (perhaps because they had a champion threat with Timothy Goebel) so that Evgeni had to come to the competition a day late. I had no idea of it was true, but my visa process was going so slowly, we weren't sure if I'd make the Russian Grand Prix at all.

Although the entire U.S. team and the rest of the international skaters had already left, I continued to train in Paris, trying not to let geopolitics divert me from my run-throughs, until finally, two days before the Grand Prix, my mother came tearing into the hotel as if she were being chased by a couple of gendarmes: she had our visas!

We were ready to go—our bags had been packed and waiting for two days. Now we just needed a flight. The U.S. Figure Skating Association travel agent could book us on a direct flight the next morning from Charles De Gaulle for Sheremetyevo on Aeroflot, but at the time the Russian airline's fleet of old planes had more than its fair share of crashes. So we took a pass and opted instead for a Lufthansa flight that connected in Frankfurt.

When we landed in Frankfurt the following day after a little hopper flight, Team Johnny was a little weary from the drama. Priscilla, my mom, and I sat silently in our own little world as we waited on the tarmac for the plane to debark. We sat and sat and sat and sat until eventually the pilot got on the intercom to say that our gate had experienced some sort of mishap and it would take hours for us to get off the plane.

We missed our flight to Moscow.

After a night in a hideous airport hotel in Frankfurt, where terrorist cells were certainly forming and I didn't sleep a wink, we left for Russia, landing (after a snow delay, of course) just in time for me to make the draw party that decided the order of skaters the next day. I wasn't on the official ice in Russia until the practice hour the morning before the competition, which left me feeling totally unprepared and terrified. Already a control freak who likes to have his skates laced and tight half an hour before I perform, I wanted everything to be absolutely perfect since this was my first time returning to Russia since 2002, when I'd withdrawn from the same event, claiming I was "sick."

The scheduling screwup was the last thing I needed for an event that would take all my confidence to win. Russia is a rough place for foreigners to compete. Not only is figure skating one of the country's most popular sports, but in general their nationalism is off the charts and makes American pride look downright unpatriotic. From a very early age, Russians are taught that they are the best. Representing America, I was already at a severe disadvantage and the lack of practice time didn't help.

But when I got on the ice, a small weary speck in the middle of this massive Soviet-built stadium called Luzhniki filled to the last row, I was treated to a wholly unexpected surprise. Huge banners with "Johnny We Love You" and "We've Been Waiting for You" written in Cyrillic letters waved in time to chants of support. The Russians welcomed me like one of their own. Tarasova, the grand doyenne of the skating world and a living legend in her native land, waited at the boards in her large fur poncho, physical proof that she stood by me.

The audience pushed me through a few mistakes and, before the last run of the straight-line footwork sequence in my long program, screamed and clapped to the music. Just like in Japan, I was floored by the fan response, although in Russia the experience was even more special because after all these years of trying to speak Russian, understand the culture, and take the best from their history of skating, its people, in a rare show of affection, accepted my performance. I wasn't perfect and got second, by a wide margin, to Evgeni Plushenko, world champion, Olympic silver medalist, and not a bad person to lose to.

The night after the Russian Grand Prix exhibition skate, I was ready to celebrate. I had the highest point total of any skater on the circuit, which meant going into my first Grand Prix Final, two weeks later in China, I was number one in the world. But first I needed to get my drink on. The Ukraina Hotel, where all the skaters were staying, one of seven famous Stalinist buildings known as the Seven Sisters, was incredibly high, incredibly old, and incredibly rundown. It didn't have computer access, the TV only received two channels, and you had to shower on your knees in the bathtub. But the grand hotel, with twenty-foot ceilings in every room including the bathrooms, was tailor-made for debauchery.

Sitting in one of the hotel's many bars, surrounded by friends I had made during summers training with Tarasova, I treated everyone, including myself, to champagne. A heavy cloud of smoke hung over the room's thick red curtains and red velvet chairs as the drink went immediately to my head. I was rail thin, hadn't touched alcohol since the Grand Prix started, and was already giddy from my current standing on the circuit. The combination made for a pretty cheerful evening.

At a certain point I spotted Evan Lysacek with a few other Americans sitting in the corner and decided to approach him in a moment of good sportsmanship.

"Having a good night, Evan?" I asked.

He wasn't a fan of Russia and had placed fifth in the event, so I didn't imagine it was the time of his life.

"Yeah, great," he said.

"I think it would be a good idea to have a handstand contest," I said out of the blue. I was pretty tipsy.

"You're on."

Upstairs in the hallway on the floor where all the Americans were staying, Evan and I competed in handstands. I was losing terribly when I came down wrong on one of my very pointy gray leather boots (I enjoy a pointy shoe because I've got small feet, and I think pointy shoes make them look bigger). In retrospect, it wasn't the most practical footwear in which to carry on a handstand contest. With a sprained ankle, I decided to call it a night and hobbled back to my room.

Getting on the bus to the airport at four o'clock the next

morning, I winced at the pain in my ankle. I was still a little tipsy from the night before and reasoned the pain, which I kept to myself, wasn't all that bad. I'd be fine by the time we landed in the States. But the tipsy feeling wore off during a deep sleep on the bus ride. And when I awoke, my ankle was so stiff I couldn't put any weight on it. Trying to get off the bus with my two giant suitcases, a small rolling bag, a purse, *and* my throbbing ankle, I ended in a jumble on the snowy street. The injury was so bad I knew I would never make it to the Grand Prix finale in China.

"Mom, I'm out. I can't. I can't," I said, covered in snow like an idiot. "I hurt my ankle . . . doing handstands."

My mom just looked at me and said, "Oh, Johnny."

Waiting for my turn in the exhibition skate after the 2005 World Championships in Moscow, I sucked fiercely on a cough drop to try to rid myself of the taste of bitter disappointment. I had worked so hard to create a special Russian number for the exhibition—the gala of champions where the top five finishers from every event performed one last time for the crowd—because I went into the competition thinking I would earn gold and become the best skater in the world. In the end, I hadn't even earned a medal.

I had returned to Moscow for the event in March cockier than ever, having just won my second national title, which firmly crowned me the best skater in America. Going into the National Championships in Portland, Oregon, as the favorite, the pressure was intense. Winning a national title is one thing, but defending it is quite another. The stress was two hundred times greater than anything I had ever experienced. The media hounded me, hoping, praying, and waiting for me to say something stupid like I had the year before.

I just kept my head down, training harder and harder and harder every day. It paid off: I beat Timothy and Evan to become the first person in several years to win two national titles in a row, and I was only twenty years old.

Going to the World Championships, in one of my adopted home cities, no less, everything was amazing. A few people waited for me at the airport, which is really rare for Russia. And some of my fans from Japan traveled to Moscow to watch me compete. Skinny from months of hard dieting and even harder workouts and fortified by my clear international support, I was ready to be world champion.

And then, a few days before the competition, my body decided to rebel.

I've always had trouble with the bottom of my foot where a calcium deposit flares up on occasion. The condition, known as sesamoiditis, is unpredictable and embarrassingly painful. As an ice skater, there is so much pressure on your body when you land that everything has to work properly or it hurts like hell. Even a toenail that's a tiny bit too long can kill.

By the third day of practices, I just couldn't pull myself together and the pain had shot up into my knee. I considered withdrawing but couldn't stand cutting short the best season of my life because of a goddamn calcium deposit. So I said, "Fuck you, foot," and tried to forget the hurt and just do my job.

I was so nervous because, if nothing else, I didn't want to let my audience down. After Evgeni withdrew because of a bad back, the Russian media told me, "Johnny, you're the highest 'Russian' right now." No pressure. Apart from the American doctor, Priscilla, and my mom, nobody knew about my sesamoiditis—it's not exactly a sexy injury—plus in figure skating, people could care less if you are hurt. If you make excuses for bad skating, you just come off as a whiner. You might have suffered a concussion or your dog just died, but all that matters is your performance on the ice.

And mine did not total up to world champion material. Skating on what felt like knives plunging into my left foot, I made some sad mistakes (like falling on my ass during a triple axel) during the short program. Though I tried to claw my way back during the free skate, with the entire Soviet stadium clapping along to the beat of my music, I couldn't pull off a world medal. Evan bumped me out of third place.

As fourth in the world, I was still able to perform my exhibition number conceived as a thank-you to the Russian people for all their support and kindness. I had decided to skate to Russian music, a radical choice since even Russian athletes wouldn't skate to their own country's music, preferring to bow to the English-speaking world in this one regard.

I chose the famous song *"Ya Tebya Ne Kogda, Ne Zabudu"* from Russia's first rock musical, *Yunona I Avos,* which told the story of Conchita, a Mexican princess, and Nikolai, a Russian naval officer who falls in love with her. Although Conchita has an arranged marriage planned, the two people from very different worlds enter into a crazy love affair. Nikolai, eventually choosing duty over love, returns to the navy, where he promptly dies in a storm, and his soul enters the body of a seagull. A hopeless romantic, I love these sad stories where one lover dies and the other one never gets over it.

The packed crowd was already in a great mood when I got on the ice, screaming and clapping for the terrific skating that made them love the sport in the first place. Their boisterous energy invigorated me: it was time to put on a show.

A hush descended while the first few melancholy chords of the sad slow song started up, and I could tell nobody grasped what the music was. They never expected an American to skate to a Russian song, so even though they had heard the song a million times, in those beginning seconds, they didn't get it.

Then the first word of the song floated over the stadium.

"Tiy."

As soon as the audience comprehended the Russian word for "you," the entire building erupted.

They loved it. Hundreds of Russian people were on fire—on their feet, screaming, cheering, crying, yelling "Bravo!" I had wanted to make a connection but the emotion was far more than I could have ever anticipated. What I didn't know at the time was the singer, Nikolai Karachentsov, a really famous artist in Russia, had just been in a bad car accident and lay in a coma at the hospital while I skated. The tragedy gave meaning and pathos to my performance.

For me, the moment had meaning of an entirely different sort. With goose bumps traveling the length of my body, I no longer cared that I was fourth. I felt so good on the ice, because people related to what I was saying with my music and movements. *"Ya tebya ne kogda, ne zabudu,"* Karachintsev sang, "I will never forget you." The reaction from the audience—which understood my artistry on the ice and desire to bridge cultural divides—was worth gold to me.

My dad, John Weir, pushing me around in diva fashion, circa mid-'80s.

My all-time favorite Halloween ~ok—Baby Bird, handcrafted y Patti Weir, circa mid-'80s, ennsylvania.

Ballet fingers at eighteen months, 1985, Pennsylvania.

Celebrating with
Shadow, 1990s,
Pennsylvania.

With my pairs partner, Jodi,
enjoying virgin daiquiris,
1997, California.

Family portrait, 2002,
Pennsylvania.

With my heroes,
Russian superstars
Maxim Marinin, Irina
Slutskaya, and Tatiana
Totmianina, autumn
2005, Moscow.

...adent
...ndings at the
...Olympic Games,
...ry 2006, Torino.

...midst of the Champions on Ice tour with my friends Irina Slutskaya, Evgeni
...nko, Tatiana Totmianina, and Marina Anissina, July 2006, Minnesota.

With my Ukrainian family, Nina Petrenko and Galina Zmievska, autumn 2007, Washington.

Patti and I in Red Square, November 2007. The Moore side of my family doesn't believe in dressing warm!

My favorite place in this world: Saint Basil's Cathedral in Red Square, November 2007.

18

my dearest friends,
der Uspenski, and I,
2007, Everett.

Paris and I having a
moment, August
2009, New York City.

With my mama at the fi[rst]
screening of my film, *P[oor?]
Star on Ice,* June 2009, [New]
York City. *(Courtesy of Sha[nnon]*
O'Neill Photography)

A quiet moment with my
agentress, Tara Modlin,
February 2010.

official badge for 2010
mpic team selection,
nuary 2010, Washington.

The tunnel leading
to the opening
ceremony of the
2010 Olympic
Winter Games,
February 2010,
Vancouver.

likely duo:
d Evan
ek at the
uver
ic Games,
ary 2010.

The first meeting with a man r[...]
parents brought me up listenin[...]
Sir Elton John, March 2010, L[...]
Angeles.

Costume fitting in New York,
summer 2010.

The original album cove[...]
for my single, "Dirty Lov[...]
(Courtesy of John Paul Tran a[...]
MAC Cosmetics)

8

Birdbrain

Harp chords, gentle as raindrops on a placid pond, and a lofting soulful cello resonated over the tinny loudspeakers of a nowheresville ice arena. A Russian legend sang *"tak krasivo, moy lebed"* ("so beautiful, my swan," as a young American skater soared and spiraled across a giant sheet of mirrored ice, re-imagining the iconic performance of Maya Plisetskaya as the Dying Swan.

I was back in Simsbury, Connecticut, that June, creating programs with Tatiana Tarasova for my first Olympic season as an actual contender, the dream I'd had since stepping on the ice at age twelve. I finally agreed to a radical idea she had been proposing since the first year we started working together. I would skate a short program to "The Swan," by Saint-Saëns, a classical piece traditionally reserved for women.

A strict and aggressive coach, Tarasova is an artist before she's anything else and sees things in a very different light than most other coaches. She relishes the over-the-top and theatrical in everything from choreography to costuming. Driven by an idealized art form in her head, she comes up with concepts that are off-the-chart crazy for skating. And my skating to "The Swan" was one of them. To her, it made perfect aesthetic sense; my naturally quiet and delicate way on the ice mirrored the mellow cello piece.

Before, I had hesitated to play the part of a dancing female swan. My public image at that point, while not exactly that of a choirboy, still retained a purity and classiness. I was a young, fragile, porcelain-looking American who stood out because I skated more like a ballet dancer. But that's where it ended. Gender bending would take me into a whole new and very taboo arena, where I would stand totally alone.

It's kind of funny, but although everyone on the outside thinks of figure skating as the gayest sport in the universe, those who wield power within it rail against that image. Female or male, skaters are supposed to represent a sanitized ideal, like a figurine atop a child's birthday cake. The result is that homosexual skaters are terrified of announcing or showing any signs of their sexual orientation since the judges, many of whom are gay themselves, will hold it against them. No American skaters were out, in public anyway, and hadn't been since U.S. champion Rudy Galindo came out publicly in 1996 after intense media pressure. The U.S. Figure Skating Association wanted it to stay that way, and even skating in a "feminine" way was tantamount in their rule book to declaring yourself gay. One had to act like a man. On skates and in sparkles.

When Tarasova initially broached the subject, I worried that skating to a piece of music traditionally reserved for women might hurt my reputation with the judges. For the Olympics, I had to release something great and memorable, so when she brought up the idea again, I reconsidered: the short program would be subtle and at the same time shocking. Four years before, Tarasova had created revolutionary programs that helped Alexei Yagudin win the Olympics. *This woman knows how to make an Olympic moment,* I thought. Putting my future in her bejeweled hands, I dove into the part of a lady swan.

As soon as we started to choreograph *The Swan,* I knew I had made the right decision. The experience was complete magic. There were times where I seemed to be running across the ice for hours on my toe picks, my arms fluttering like the feathers of a wounded swan. Tarasova stripped me down to the basest, most animalistic elements of a bird, and on that freeing journey, we were so pleased with ourselves we began calling the program a "masterpiece." Perhaps a little cocky, but swans aren't known for their humility.

I spent all summer preening my new feathers and giving interviews in which I talked about *The Swan*'s great beauty and originality. By its debut at my first Grand Prix event of the year in Canada that October, however, I had shed a lot of my initial certainty. There was big pressure at Skate Canada, the first real international event of the Olympic season, and *The Swan* had gone through drastic choreography changes from the original to conform to new amendments to the judging system the International Skating Union had voted on late that summer. They altered the parameters of acceptable spins and step sequences in a way that forced skaters to jam in more technique (and leave behind any art) in order to rack up points. My poor swan aside, the season leading up to the Olympics was a pretty stressful time to be changing the rules.

At the practice for the Grand Prix, I could already feel the first blush of Olympic fever. In Canada, they're crazy about skating, and fans, who had paid for tickets just to watch the practices, packed the building. I wore my swan costume (I always like to warm up in my costume before the real event) under a jacket but was unabashedly excited to let this beauty free. Feathers delicately etched from sequins and stitching extended across my torso, a few floating freely and dramatically down my black pant leg. One arm, representing the long neck of a swan, cleverly ended in a red glove that looked like a swan's beak. The other arm, covered in sparkling netting, was an avant-garde nod to the under layer in the construction of a swan costume and the deep ballet tradition of this piece.

Before I had a chance to ditch the jacket, a few of the Russian officials came up to Priscilla and me, kissing us warmly on both our cheeks and slapping our backs with loving roughness. They were especially keen on seeing me do well at the Grand Prix.

"Everyone's looking to you to carry America at the Olympics," they said. "Evgeni Plushenko, Stéphane Lambiel, and you are the favorites."

Their words thrilled like a juicy piece of surprising gossip. But then their high praise was quickly supplanted with an opposite reaction. Was *my* country looking to me to carry our men's team at the Olympics? The news came as a shock since my federation had never shown me anything close to that sentiment. It was confusing. But no matter my federation's plan for the future, the Russians had jolted me back into excitement to show in this moment what I could do as The Swan.

I took off my warm-up jacket with hundreds of pairs of eyes watching my every move and cast my glance downward to get deep into the mind-set of a demure and sensitive bird. The audience had no idea what a treat they were in for—a real artiste on the ice. But just then I heard a strange sound, which I didn't recognize at first. It was the crowd laughing at me.

A gaggle of reporters crowded around me after an event, waiting for a famous Weir sound bite and, well, I aimed to please. Still in my swan costume, one of them asked about my one red hand. When addressing the press, I always tried to avoid the obvious and add a little something unexpected. So I didn't want to simply answer, "It's the swan's beak, dummy." Then it hit me, out of nowhere, true inspiration.

"Well, his name is Camille—two *l*'s," I said, thinking about the music's genius composer Camille Saint-Saëns. "I think he's my evil side. When I skate poorly, I blame it on my glove."

I thought it was funny, and so did the reporters. They thought a lot of stuff I said those days was funny. Since I first performed *The Swan* at Skate Canada, something in me had shifted. The moment I appeared on the ice in my swan costume was a near catastrophe that wound up spinning into a huge success. I pushed past the snickering and skated *The Swan* so well the crowd went crazy. People were initially uncomfortable with the spectacle, but the intense emotion that built and unfurled slowly, just like emotions in real life, really resonated. It foreshadowed the reality that *The Swan* would become one of my most popular programs and completely change the world's perception of me.

Unfortunately, the rest of the event didn't go nearly as well. During the free skate, I made a long series of mistakes that ended with me badly spraining my ankle. They pulled me off the ice and put my leg in a cast as I watched the hideous scores that put me in a humiliating seventh place.

Still, it was as if the bird's spirit had untethered me from my last remaining inhibitions. Both my personality and persona were in serious flux. *The Swan* took my natural inclination for poetic license and launched it into the realm of pure camp. Freeing my artistic side in a way that flew in the face of my federation's ideals transformed me from the innocent to seriously sassy in what I had to say.

I stood out all the more because most skaters limit themselves to a very boring script in the hopes of not offending anyone. In sports, there's a clear line of what you can and can't discuss. While you're supposed to bring attention to your sport, it should be in a very rah-rah American way that won't offend a Republican or Christian rights group. The federation wants little robots that all spout the same message. And I was anything but that. I refused to stick to the script: "I hope I skate well. I just want to do my best, and I've worked really hard with my coach." This boosted my popularity with people outside skating's microcosm. Regular kids watching at home adored me because I clearly didn't give a shit about what others thought. That's universal appeal.

The one irritating by-product of my liberation, however, was the media's new moniker for me: flamboyant. Whereas before they had described me as artistic and elegant, now I was "over-the-top" and, of course, "flamboyant." The sexual connotations of the word annoyed me because sex, as much as I might enjoy it, has nothing to do with how I skate. But even more than that, it implied a lack of seriousness and I was as serious as any skater out there, just not as boring. Still, there wasn't a single article about me that didn't use the f-word, and there were a lot of articles about me.

I couldn't complain too much since I was complicit in my new "flamboyant" image. It was like a drug: the more outrageous I sounded, the more attention I got. I gave the people what they wanted with loose comments like:

—declaring myself a "country bumpkin"

—describing my outfit as a "Care Bear on acid"

—calling skating judges "furry old women sitting there with grimaces on their faces"

My colorful language made me the clear press, and public, favorite. But my federation was not pleased. The Loose Cannon had become a fey loose cannon. I was basically their worst nightmare.

By the National Championships in January (the biggest deciding event of my career to that point because of its direct impact on the Olympic team), they let it be known that Evan Lysacek, my main American rival, was the favorite of U.S. Figure Skating Association officials. They spread the word at the event held in Saint Louis that it was Evan's time to win. Their claim wasn't baseless; his Grand Prix season had been stellar, whereas mine had not. But his skating was less of a factor than his persona. For figure skating people, he was easier to get their heads around. Straitlaced, he did everything they told him to. Meanwhile, I was out there wearing a swan carcass.

Although the press loved me because I was open and entertaining, and the public was ready to crown me the star of the upcoming Olympics, as the federation promoted Evan as skating's newest angel, I could feel myself getting pushed out. And I didn't like it.

My only weapon in the war for the halo was a performance that nobody could quibble with. Fueled by the fire of a scorned skater, I performed one of the best programs of my career. My *Swan* at the Nationals was stunning, with not one move or element out of place, earning me a personal best score of 83.28, the highest recorded for a short program in the United States under the new judging system at that time. Evan and Michael Weiss both fell, so I finished the night with a huge lead ahead of second place.

I celebrated by making a really off-color drug reference to the crowd of reporters waiting for me when I got off the ice that compared my performance to another skater's speedier program.

"For [mine], they kind of sat back and had their cognac and their cigarettes and they were relaxing and watching," I said. "His was like a vodka-shot-let's-snort-coke kind of thing."

The federation was fuming the next morning when my comment popped up in countless newspaper articles and Internet postings. While I practiced in the day off between the short and long program, one of the federation's biggest bosses pulled me aside.

"The other skater's mother is very upset and wants you to make a public apology to him," he said. "You have completely disrespected U.S. figure skating, and you need to fix it."

"Really?"

Of course, I didn't fix it. I didn't care. I mean, it was just a little comment, not a big life-or-death issue. This wasn't a communist country; I was free to say what I liked.

Going into my long program with that defiant, and naive, stance, I quickly lost my eleven-point lead to a bunch of technicalities (and my big mouth). Although I had the crowd on its feet, I had done too many combinations according to the new rules, so I received no points for one jumping pass.

After a few nail-biting moments of watching the guys behind me skate, I won the National Championship for the third year in a row, something nobody had done since Brian Boitano in the '80s. But I considered the win tarnished by what I saw as an unjustly small margin. Still, no one outside the skating world cares about points, only winners and losers. With three national titles under my belt and a direct pass to the Olympics, it appeared to the public like I was forever dominant over U.S. figure skating. Far from the truth, I was more than happy to let that image prevail.

My win at the Nationals immediately launched me into the frenzy of the Olympic season, when the whole world, which hasn't paid attention to skating for four years, suddenly tunes in. My name was everywhere, and everyone started calling and coming out of the woodwork. Suddenly we needed a security guard at the front of my rink (which blacked out all of its windows because of the attention) because people were sneaking in to watch me or get on-ice interviews. In between training every day, I was on the phone with different media outlets like *Sports Illustrated* and the *New York Times* so that when people discussed U.S. figure skating at the Olympics, it wasn't the great ice dancers Tanith Belbin and Ben Agosto they talked about, or even Sasha Cohen. It was Johnny Weir. Despite what my federation thought, the press and public had crowned me the next princess of the Olympic Games.

9

Golden Boy

Priscilla and I prepared to go through a third security checkpoint to get into the Olympic Village in Torino, which was more secure than an army base. I hoisted my enormous Rimowa suitcases onto a table for an Italian policeman to inspect. He dexterously maneuvered around the cases and started rifling through the furs, black jeans, boots, and colorful scarves I had brought for my first trip to the Olympics.

When he finished, a few national police waved us forward with their large machine guns. Then we boarded a bus that would finally take us into the Village, but not before the policemen checked underneath, using long sticks with mirrors on the ends, to make sure there were no bombs. Because of the atrocity against the Israeli team by Black September, a Palestinian terrorist organization back during the Munich games of 1972, the Olympics had become something of a militarized zone.

The alarming experience of entering the fortified gate exacerbated my prior reservations about staying in the Olympic Village. When competing, I'm one to be very alone, and in the Olympics it's typical to have four roommates per bedroom. My biggest fear was being housed in a room with four other skaters that I'd be competing against. We would bump into each other on the way to the single shower and pass the flu around, another common occurrence at the games.

But as soon as we made it past the guards, the heaviness lifted. I saw the flags with the Olympic rings flutter against Torino's mellow rolling landscape. Fresh-faced athletes from around the world walked along little pathways to the various buildings, and instinctively I felt the sheer joy and excitement of being part of this elite group.

My happiness only increased upon learning of my housing assignment: a single room in the same condo as the curling team's doctors and coaches. My federation had granted me my wish by putting me far away from the other skaters. Priscilla and I split up (she was staying with the female skating team), and I entered the curling house, hauling my heavy, heavy luggage up three flights to my own private floor.

I opened the door onto the sad little scene. Despite the European obsession with thread count and hand tailoring, I always find their accommodations pretty mean. There was a twin-sized wooden bed frame, with a thin mattress covered by a blue fleece blanket on it. Next to it, a little brown stool functioned as a side table. The only closet was a small wardrobe that wouldn't even house the furs I had brought along. A tile floor with no rugs added the final chilling detail.

Because I spend so much of my time on the road, there's nothing I hate more than checking into a hotel room and having it feel very foreign. I need my home base to have a security-blanket feel in order to withstand the harsh realities of training and competing. This monastic chamber as it stood would not do as my lodging for the next three weeks.

I walked over to Priscilla's room to check out her living space, but when I arrived she was nowhere to be found. The building was empty since the women's skating team didn't arrive for another week and a half. So I started poking around and a lightbulb went off in my head. I grabbed a bunch of fleece blankets, two lamps, a bedside table, and a few extra towels for good measure. Laden down with all my loot, I shimmied across the Olympic Village and into the curling quarters.

Back in my room, I set to work decorating my space. I lifted the bed up, which only took about two fingers because it was so light, and I spread out two of the blue fleece blankets as a rug that almost covered the entire floor space. I unpacked, staging my luggage for a touch of glamour. I hung my fur coats on the door handles for coziness and my official accreditation on the wall for inspiration. I arranged framed photos of me, my family,

Alex, and my dog and lastly lit a few candles. By the time I got into bed, I felt at home.

"Johnny, the smalls were running out but we put some aside because we knew you were coming," an Olympic official said before handing me three enormous bags of Team USA paraphernalia. In the team processing area, where I received my information and uniforms for the Olympics, I wondered how I was going to fit all this stuff into my already cramped room.

Me being me, I knew I wasn't really going to wear any of the uniforms the smiling woman handed me. I don't believe in them and for years had gotten in trouble for it. That whole tracksuit look; it's just not me. Simply put, they're tacky. I'm very proud to be American but I don't feel the need to rub it in everyone's face with an ugly jacket. I wear what I want, which is usually black and fun. Isn't freedom as American as apple pie and football?

Although I didn't like to wear team uniforms, the processing was a proud moment. As soon as the woman handed me my bags that she had held especially for me, I felt like a real part of the U.S. team. And that was something I hadn't felt before, either, because of my federation's slights or because I had excluded myself. I threw myself into the Olympic spirit and into the entire uniform to the delight of the photographers who snapped my picture. I had worked long and hard for this goal; it was time to enjoy it.

That first photo op and subsequent press conference was a continuation of the love affair between me and the press. During the media event with the rest of the men's team, Evan Lysacek, Matthew Savoie, and myself, nearly every single question was directed at me.

"Johnny, how are you preparing for the Olympics?"

"Ambien and espresso."

Laughs.

"How are you enjoying the Olympic Village?"

"It's dirty. I had to do a lot of cleaning."

More laughs.

I was more than pleased to be the ringleader of this American team of young, talented, first-time Olympians. However, the microscope I was under didn't lose its focus after the press conference. Lots of media showed up for every official practice held for the male single skaters. In addition to the judges and other skaters watching, it made for a tough training situation. I didn't want people to see me sweat or breathe heavily. And I certainly didn't want to fall on my ass and have it appear in every newspaper the next day with the headline: "Weir Not Olympic Ready!" So for a week and a half, I didn't push myself in an effort to appear perfect, and my condition started to go down.

To blow off steam in this pressure-cooker environment, I engaged in massive retail therapy in downtown Torino. I let the conversion rate unnecessarily confuse me into thinking everything was cheaper than it was and made very good friends with the people at Louis Vuitton. I went to their boutique practically every day even if I just got a wallet or a little bracelet. Personally imitating a housewife working out her emotions with her credit card at the mall, I spent way too much money that Olympics.

There weren't enough monogrammed LVs in the world, however, to soothe my nerves the day I finally had to compete in the short program. My anxiety scared me (I hadn't felt crazy like that since I was a junior skater) even though my expectations were tempered going into the competition. With Evgeni Pluskenko and Stéphane Lambiel skating, I wasn't sure I would even place. But this was the Olympics. Billions of people would be watching and that alone sent me spinning.

I pushed through my day, practicing and then heading into the city for a simple plate of salad that I ate by myself. Then I returned to my room where I watched *Will & Grace* (God, I love that Karen) on my portable DVD player before taking a nap. Not wanting to be rushed, I began putting on my makeup and doing my hair two hours before it was time to catch the bus to the arena.

Right before I left my room, I said a little prayer asking whoever is up there to help me: *give me power, put air in my lungs, and just help me push.* I blew my candles out and went downstairs to meet Priscilla.

Backstage at the rink, it was dark and crammed with people. I frantically searched for a place to hide and collect my thoughts, but every nook seemed occupied with skaters, coaches, press, and volunteers. Although newly built for the Olympics, the place stunk of sweat, leather, ammonia, and fear. I felt like I couldn't breathe.

Then time ran out. I walked out of the tunnel and into light so bright it was blinding. There were so many people, so many TV cameras, so many photographers. Dark circular lenses almost ringed the entire rink.

As my eyes adjusted to the light, the announcer said my name and I thought the roof would blow off the building with the American, Russian, and Japanese fans all cheering for me.

I knew it was this Olympic moment for which I had created the *The Swan,* and a lot of things were going to happen in the next ten minutes.

Although my feet were on the ice, my mind floated up to the fans in the seats and returned backstage. Then it settled on the issue of my less-than-perfect condition. In my attempt to maintain a perfect image during practices for the past couple of weeks, I hadn't done full run-throughs of either my short or long program. For as good a shape I was in going into the Olympics, I hadn't kept it up in the period right up to the event.

I had to snap myself back into the moment, right here, right now, on the ice. So I moved toward the boards and punched the wall so hard my knuckles went red and hurt like hell. That did the trick. As I moved onto the ice, the arena went completely quiet. Nobody was screaming; nobody was talking. All I could hear were the shutters on all the cameras around the rink going off. I stood, in the middle of the sporting world, alone on a giant sheet of white ice.

My music started and I completely zoned out the camera shutters, bright lights, flags, and people. Concentrating on the chords of the harp that began the piece, I just started to skate the way that I knew I could. I let the music carry me through my first jump, a triple axel—flawless. Then my second, triple lutz-triple toe—also flawless. I followed it with a perfect sit spin, and people began to cheer. For a spin! I nailed the footwork sequence and began skating full speed toward my last jump.

I was making eye contact with the judges—trying to pick out the ones I knew so I could give them an extra-soulful dying-swan look before going into the jump—when suddenly I realized that—*Oh, my God!*—I was doing the wrong footwork. At that time, I trained with Priscilla each morning by doing different entrances into jumps and had mixed myself up.

With the wall rapidly approaching, I had to do something, so I just jumped. *The Swan* provided, and I landed the triple flip perfectly, did one more beautiful spin into a balletic step sequence and my final combination spin. The crowd roared while I tucked into my last I'm-a-dead-swan pose.

I shrugged as I got off the ice. It had been a clean performance, but the botched footwork left me wanting something more from myself. It certainly wasn't as good as the National Championships. What an inane mistake at the end! I waited for disappointment.

Then the marks came up. Up until that point, my highest international score had been around 75, a pretty average sum. For my Olympic performance of *The Swan,* I earned a total of 80 points, putting me in second place behind Plushenko and ahead of Lambiel and the Canadian skater Jeffrey Buttle. I literally couldn't believe it.

If the hard numbers didn't do it, the excitement from everyone backstage drove home the reality that I was the only American in a position to win a medal. Evan had placed tenth by the end of the night and the next American was a few behind him. My whole team patted me on the back, congratulating me for carrying our country. Every reporter, even ones that I'd had some friction with in the past, were there, too, smiling and proud. They lobbed me softball questions, which were basically all different forms of "How does it feel to be so awesome?"

It felt great, and it only got better when I returned to my room. Emails from fans in the United States and around the world filled my account. They had come in almost as soon as I finished the competition. "Johnny, you are America's bright star." "We love you, Johnny!" "I want you to marry my daughter—you two even look alike!" Okay, some of them were a little off, but the incredible outpouring of love and support covered me like a warm blanket as I drifted off to a contented sleep.

———————

The night before the long program, I couldn't sleep at all. I couldn't come down from the idea that by the end of tomorrow, less than ten years into my skating career, I might have my first Olympic medal. Tossing and turning on the paper-thin mattress,

I was having heart palpitations. So many people were waiting for me to win it. What if I let them down? I couldn't; I was too close. But of course I could—I had choked for much less before. As the first light of morning filtered in through the window, the ceiling and walls seemed to close in on me.

It was going to be a very long and lonely day. After my morning practice, attended by every person with press credentials and a pulse, I had a hideous amount of time to kill before the competition, which wasn't until late at night so that it could be televised live in the States.

To get away from my panicky thoughts, I watched a *Will & Grace* marathon, letting the narcotic of TV lull me into a much-needed nap in which I slept harder than I had in months. When I awoke, I started in slowly on the routine that had proved successful for the short program, spending an inordinate amount of time on my hair and makeup, saying my prayer, blowing out my candles, and walking downstairs to meet Priscilla and the bus that would take us to the competition.

Priscilla and I, both bundles of nerves wrapped in heavy furs, didn't speak as we stood waiting at the bus stop. The only other sign of life in the dark, quiet, cold and completely dead Olympic Village was the president of the Japan Skating Federation, who waited next to us for the bus. The three of us watched our breath make little silent clouds against the sky for a while. Then Priscilla pulled her hand out of her coat to check her watch. The Japanese president and I gave her a sideways glance but stayed silent. A few seconds later Priscilla checked her watch again.

"Do you know where the bus is?" Priscilla asked the president.

"No. It's supposed to be now," she answered.

After checking her watch once more, Priscilla startled the small Japanese woman with her loud, nervous laugh. The bus, scheduled to be here at half past the hour, was now ten minutes late and we officially started to freak out. How were we going to get to the rink? It wasn't like there were cabs or subways in the Olympic Village.

"Oh, well. I guess nobody wants me to skate," I joked nervously.

Nobody laughed. Priscilla walked out into the middle of the deserted street while the president wrung her hands. All of a sudden Priscilla began flapping her arms like a crazy duck. A pair of headlights appeared in the distance.

A volunteer, on call for emergencies, pulled up in a tiny Smart car. While the emergencies were supposed to be things like slipping on the ice or suicide bombers, we begged her to take us to the rink. We piled into the minuscule automobile, skating equipment, furs, limbs, and all, and drove like bats out of hell to get there on time.

When we arrived, every TV camera was waiting for me because I was supposed to be on the bus that had emptied out twenty minutes earlier (apparently we were the only ones who hadn't received the memo that the bus schedule had changed that day). They all quickly cut to my awkward extrication from this clown car, but I could have cared less. I ran into the building so I could get my spot in the dressing room and start getting ready.

There is nothing I hate more than being rushed—but I really hated it at the Olympics. Everything was go-go-go from that moment on. I got into my costume, laced up my skates, and prepared to walk out of the chute and into the warm-up. If I found the crowd during the short program loud, it was nothing compared to the deafening noise that night. In the final group, there were six men skating from six different countries: Russia, America, Switzerland, Japan, Canada, and France. The result was an international cacophony that defied comprehension. The Swiss had cowbells, the French had horns, and everyone had guttural or high-pitched screams in their native languages.

As a performer, you love to hear the audience cheering. But this was aggressive to the point of overwhelming. It was so loud Priscilla had to yell things to me while we stood face-to-face. In this most important moment of my life, I couldn't hear my coach; I couldn't even hear myself.

I didn't hear them call my name, but when the third skater finished I knew it was my time to compete. The lighting was dimmer than it had been for the short program, almost like relaxing mood lighting. But I was so tight that I couldn't feel the ice. It's important to me that my feet are one with the ice, but in that moment I was keenly aware of being on top of it.

I moved on full autopilot to the piano in "Otoñal." After completing three jumping passes and a spin perfectly, I started getting into the groove and enjoying the audience's amplification with each element.

There was a bit of a breather in my program before skating into my second triple axel, and in that momentary void of activity, I lost focus. I looked around and remembered my stiffness, bringing that quality to the next jump. I didn't finish the rotation and landed on two feet. My incomplete triple axel set me off for a shaky footwork sequence. Before the next element, a combination jump of a triple lutz and a triple toe loop, I tried to snap myself back into my performance. But because I was so nervous I wouldn't make it, I just did the triple lutz and left more points on the table.

The next couple of jumps were fine, and running through my head was the thought: *Okay, Johnny, you've definitely fucked up enough. Get it together.* I skated toward the judges for the last jump, but as I was setting up I tripped and had to skate right through. I was so shocked by the whole situation that I couldn't remember what mistakes I had made already in the four-and-a-half-minute program. Like a goldfish swimming around in a circle, I forgot what I'd done and where I'd been. I knew, however, I couldn't leave all those points from a second missed jump, so in that second I changed my program. I turned around, heading in completely the wrong direction, and tried to jump again. And I did it, although it was really ugly, and I barely landed it.

I moved to the kiss and cry area in a daze. Devastated that I hadn't fought for the program and instead let myself and everyone down, all I wanted to do was cry. But with three billion people watching me around the world, I had to keep the tears bottled up. A few did escape when the number five popped up next to my name on the monitor in front of me. That was it. No suspense. No second chance. I flat out didn't have a medal.

In the mix zone, where the media interviews the athletes, the press eagerly awaited my arrival. But for a different reason than I was used to.

"How do you feel now that you've lost America's medal?" a reporter shouted.

I had lost an Olympic medal, the only thing that I really wanted and the reason I started skating in the first place. I felt awful. Talking right now was going to be difficult, but I didn't realize just how difficult.

"What happened today?" another said.

"I missed the bus to come here, which got me off on the wrong foot. I felt rushed at the arena because I was late," I said.

As soon as the words came out of my mouth, I realized I had made one of the biggest media flubs of my career.

"You're blaming a botched triple toe loop on the bus?" a reporter asked.

"No, I was just saying that I spent the day doing my makeup and then I missed the bus, so—"

"So you missed the bus because you were doing your makeup?"

I was getting twisted in my own words. The clever Johnny who also skated well had left the building. I knew I had skated poorly and was the first person to say so, but they thought I was making excuses, and nobody likes excuses. The American press that had loved me so much the day before, and the day before that, and the month before that, started to turn.

"There's a poll on the Internet asking whether people care whether you are gay or not. What's your response?"

What a perfect time to bring up my sexuality. I had to get the fuck out of there; this was starting to get ugly (I didn't realize it then but something a lot uglier awaited me back in my room. I received hate mail from many of the same people who had earlier sent me fan mail. "You failed the country. You failed us." And that was a nice letter. "You wear animals; you should die." "You lost our medal; you should die." One letter even hoped that I'd get "raped to death.")

Priscilla extricated me from the press conference from hell. As we walked back to the dressing room, I stopped to check the drug-testing list. The skaters who placed first, second, and third had mandatory drug testing. And then there was one random test—and of course it was me. What did I do to deserve this? I threw my water bottle against the wall and it burst everywhere. Walking into the locker room to change out of my costume, I practically ripped the gorgeous velvet and net creation off my emaciated shoulders, growling at no one in particular. I was a livid, crestfallen failure. This was not the Olympic moment I had wanted.

I was the first one in the antidoping room since I was the only one who didn't have to participate in the awards ceremony. Wearing their medals, Evgeni, Stéphane, and Jeffrey were excitedly talking with their coaches as they walked in about forty-five minutes later. On the American team, skaters aren't allowed to have their coach with them during drug tests, so I was all alone staring at the three Olympic medalists I had lost to. I took a seat by the window and let the tears I had been holding back since my performance fall. Nobody cared; I cried without making a sound, plus they were all too engrossed to pay any attention to me.

The event had been over for a good hour and a half before I was able to leave. I had had trouble urinating because of my wrecked nerves, so everyone else, the fans, the skaters, and the officials, were already gone when I finally exited the building.

I walked outside into the complete darkness. It was pushing one o'clock and the big paved courtyard was completely deserted. The idling engine of the waiting bus lent a feeling of drudgery to the desolate scene.

"Johnny!"

I looked over, and I saw my mom. Standing behind the bars that fenced in the courtyard, she put her arms through them and out toward me.

It would have been a security breach for me to leave the official premises, so I ran over to her and we hugged with the bars between us. When I stood back I saw her glasses were all fogged up.

"I'm so sorry," I said. "I'm so sorry for all of this—what I've done to the family, and with money, and all this stuff."

"Honey, you made it to the Olympics," she said. "I've never been more proud of you in my life."

10

After the Storm

I had been to Las Vegas before, but never like this. When I was shown into the suite at Caesars Palace that Kathy Griffin's people had put me up in, it took my breath away—and I'm the biggest snob ever when it comes to hotel rooms. Four lavish rooms, bedecked with chandeliers and gobs of marble, were capped off with a giant seashell bathtub in the middle of one of the bathrooms. I was definitely going to get some much-needed rest and relaxation in these stunning surroundings.

Kathy had asked me to appear on her Bravo reality show, *My Life on the D-List*, after she saw a reference I had made to her show in a post-Olympics interview. After I'd appeared on the cover of the *New York Times* I had told a reporter at Russia House—the country's official debauched party palace in Torino—that my new widespread notoriety put me "on the same level as Kathy Griffin and her D-List." I was joking, but someone from her team called to see if I would do an episode, and Kathy herself followed up by sending flowers.

The bouquet was unnecessary (but appreciated). A huge fan of the comedian and her show, I said yes right away. While I don't get starstruck easily, Kathy Griffin was pretty A-List to me.

With a couple of hours to go before our meeting, I took a quick shower and ordered chicken fingers with ranch dressing up to the room as my first post-season treat. Nothing could soothe me after what I had been through at the Olympics—not a truckload of chicken fingers or a twenty-room suite at Caesars—but the trip offered a welcome distraction.

Of course, making my entertainment TV debut came with its own worries. I had to watch what I said and did on air. Because Kathy was a gay icon, I didn't want to give her anything too gay or over the top. In private I had no issues with my sexuality, but I still wasn't comfortable with it as a topic of public discourse. I didn't need it put all over a TV show.

And there was the issue of what to wear. The episode's setup was that I would teach Kathy how to skate. During the Olympics I'd established myself as really into fashion, so I had to look good. At the same time, I was going to be on the ice and I'd already been away from home for two weeks, so I was on the last legs of what was still clean in my luggage. I freaked out for a good hour, trying on different ensembles and running through my suite to look at myself in various gold-framed mirrors until I settled on my skater-with-an-edge look: track pants and a giant black John Galliano hoodie that zipped off to the side. It was a little aggressive for ice skating, but with my flat-ironed hair ending in a long unruly mullet, so was I.

Greeting me at the tiny rink in the middle of Las Vegas with big, loving, open arms, Kathy immediately put me at ease. She had gathered all the kids who trained at the rink to watch from above, which was a really thoughtful move. Their clapping and screaming upon my arrival made me feel like a super A-List celebrity worthy of a TV appearance.

I held Kathy's hand for what she called a "couples skate" and tried to be professional while giving her pointers for looking beautiful on the ice. "Don't use your butt," I shouted, describing her during the session as a "liver sausage" and a "monkey." Okay, maybe I was going for funny more than professional. Whatever I did, it worked. Everyone was pleased with my performance, including Kathy, who paid me the highest compliment off-air by calling me "one of her gays."

Although I still fretted over the past season, which had ended in a monumentally disappointing Olympics and my transformation into the laughingstock of the skating world, my appearance on the *D-List* was just one example of the new and massive stage that I had entered.

Love me or hate me, everyone seemed to have an opinion about me.

By no stretch of the imagination did I kid myself then (or now) that I was famous. I'm no Britney Spears with paparazzi camped outside my house or trailing me as I pick up my dry cleaning. Still, as a top athlete with the rare ability to be myself, I became an object of curiosity and entered the pop culture radar as a tiny celebrity blip.

I knew whatever fame I found would be very fleeting, so I wanted to do as many things to get my face out there as possible, particularly because my skating was shaky enough to make me worried for my future in the sport. I loved the invitations to exclusive events, such as the opening of a club in Manhattan's meatpacking district or a party to showcase Louis Vuitton's new collection, which had started arriving at the house in Delaware. But between skating, touring, having a relationship, and getting ready for a new season, there was no room for parties (plus, I'm not really a party person; I am terrible at meeting new people). Anything that resembled a work opportunity, however, I tried to make happen.

So when two different production companies approached me right after the Olympics about making a documentary of my life, I was into the idea—although I had absolutely no clue what it meant. Totally oblivious to how most of the entertainment world worked, I figured they would shoot for a couple months, make a movie, play it somewhere, and that would be it. But the first people that approached me (they had produced the popular documentary *Murderball* about quadriplegic athletes who play wheelchair rugby) quickly disabused me of that notion. They had a plan to buy the house next to the one where I lived with my parents in order to shoot everything I did from morning until night. That was a little too aggressive for my taste.

I probably would have nixed the whole idea if it weren't for Butch and Grämz—aka David Barba and James Pellerito. When they came to my rink to propose a movie about my life and career, they were upfront: they had no sponsor and no money. Their company, Retribution Media, was basically them working catering jobs on the side to fund their shoots. A couple as well as work partners, they wanted to do the doc in a very low-key way, shooting me during scheduled times when it worked for all of us. Priscilla was fine with it, as long as it didn't detract from my training. My family was also on board, and Paris "loved it."

They dove right in, coming down from New York to Delaware about once a week to film my training in hopes they could turn my antics into a movie. Because I tend to nickname people when they come into my life, even if they come with their own nicknames, I had to rename James and David before we could get down to business. David became "Butch" because he's the smaller of the two with a little faux-hawk, which gives him a bit of a tough puppy look. And what better name for a puppy than Butch? But Butch wasn't allowed to drive because he was in this country from Mexico on a green card. So James had to do all the driving, and being from New York City, he was a terrible driver, crouching up near the steering wheel of their small rental and holding on for dear life while inching along at fifty miles an hour. I crowned him "Grams" because of his grandmotherly style of driving. But he didn't appreciate his new nickname, so I had to cool it out with *z* at the end and an umlaut over the *a*—a modern Grämz that we both could live with.

While the idea of a documentary about my life took a little bit of convincing at the outset (since there were a number of things at that time, like my love life, which I didn't want aired in public), I needed no pitch—or money—when *BlackBook* asked me to do a fashion spread. The editors of the hip fashion magazine had reached out to me because they liked my kind of elfin quality to which they wanted to add the magic of designer clothes.

I was over the moon about doing my first big photo shoot, although it represented yet another break with the skating world. Most male skaters, if they get any mainstream press, it's usually a page in *Men's Health* where they talk about their awesome abs and pose in a Team USA T-shirt. Occasionally the girls will do something a little more outrageous, like when Katarina Witt posed nude for *Playboy*. For some reason, everyone's okay when the women shed their clothes for a nudie mag. However, I knew the federation would *not* be okay with my appearing in a high-fashion spread where they planned God-knows-what kind of outfits. It would embarrass and shock them. So I went ahead and booked the shoot immediately.

I had been to New York many times, but when I arrived on the train the night before the shoot it was my first trip to the big city alone. And I get nervous my first time doing anything. It didn't help that the magazine had booked me into a hotel in one of the Villages. East or West, I'm not a big Village fan. And this hotel was vintage Village—dark and dirty and small. A homeboy in big, baggy jeans that I guess was supposed to be the desk clerk showed me and my mega Rimowa suitcase (I don't pack light, even for overnight trips) to my room where I could just feel the cockroaches staring at me. When I stay at a hotel, I like there to be room service, not a woman moaning in the room next to mine.

There was no way I was staying there. Sitting on a plastic laundry bag on the bed, I started calling every famous, expensive hotel that I could think of in New York City: the Ritz-Carlton, the Four Seasons, the Plaza. Nothing. Fully booked. Finally I found a generic business hotel in midtown with a room—three stars as opposed to the negative six-star hotel I was in—and I hightailed it out of there in time to get a few hours of sleep before my 7 a.m. start time.

All was forgiven and forgotten the minute I arrived at the studio. There were hair and makeup people, a stylist, the photographer, and his assistants running around the large white loft, which was drenched with sun pouring in through enormous windows. And there were tons and tons of beautiful clothes everywhere. The glamour! It was a big-deal fashion shoot . . . for me. (Of course, I had to say something about the "hotel." "Just for your information, it was terrible," I told the editor. But in that way New York trendy people pretend nothing is a mistake, she passed it off as though they thought it would be a cool, cultural experience.)

The photographer, David Armstrong, only used natural light, which made me nervous that I wouldn't look great. But, I mean, twenty-one years old, skinny as a rail, and in love—how bad could I look?

Plus, the clothes were the real stars. I had never seen such treasures. There were Henri Duarte jeans and Wunderkind shorts, amazing rings by Etro, a Dior jacket worth $30,000 that had flown in from a fashion show in Hong Kong the night before the shoot, plus many designers I had never even heard of despite my extensive studies.

In the spread that they called "Johnny: I'm Only Dancing," it was drama, drama, drama. I flipped over one setup (which they didn't end up using in the magazine) where I portrayed the late, legendary dancer Rudolf Nureyev with the whole pancake-on-the-face ballet makeup and hair extensions in a pulled-back ponytail.

Like the Nureyev photos, the majority of the shots we did were topless. I was all for nudity. I loved having my picture taken and wanted so much to do a good job that I would have done anything. And I pretty much did. I danced across the studio and slithered on the floor. When they brought out a pair of six-inch Gucci stilettos to go with the leggings I wore, I didn't flinch, even though I knew a photo of me in ladies' heels would cause major waves in the skating world. Hey, they make anybody's legs look better. I pranced around like a high-end call girl, which emboldened the editors to put a Gucci dress on me. I tried my hardest to cram myself into the size 00 dress, but I wasn't a miracle worker. They had to settle on letting it sit like a skirt around my waist with my arms wrapped around my, of course, naked torso while I didn't breathe. What we do for beauty.

―――――

While I loved every minute of my pop culture moments, they didn't pay the bills. For that I again joined the cast of Champions on Ice in what would be my longest tour to date. From the beginning of April through August, I crisscrossed the country in a bus with the best skaters in the world, including Evan Lysacek and Stéphane Lambiel, both of whom I had lost to in the Olympics and would be once more competing against the next season.

For my number, I chose to skate to Frank Sinatra's "My Way" for its obvious symbolism. The Olympic season had nearly killed me, but at least I could hold my head up high because I had done it my way.

The actual skating is such a small part of any tour. There's a lot more traveling, waiting around, and—at least in the case of that year's Champions show—drinking. To make it through the slog of this endless tour, I drank nearly every night during dinner and lots of times while traveling on the bus. No sooner had we loaded into the bus after a performance when the Russians would whip out their bottles of vodka (or someone feeling fancy might have picked up a bottle of champagne), which we happily let them pour into our paper cups as small cities receded into the distance. I'm not a big drinker in general, but at that time, when I was superskinny from the Olympic season, I was an especially cheap date. For that spring and summer, I grew my tolerance and joined the rest of the merry band of skaters. Having a buzz made being far from home and Alex after such a rocky couple of months a little easier to swallow.

Alcohol wasn't my only solace during the tour. Marina Anissina, the 2002 Olympic Champion in ice dancing and one of my best friends, became my greatest confidante and constant dinner companion. Over absurdly glamorous meals of filet mignon or sushi (and, of course, lots of wine), I moaned to her about the clear downfall of my condition. Four months was a long time to be on the road and away from training for a competitive figure skater, but there was no other way; I needed the money if I wanted to keep skating.

So I had to strategize a way to create new programs for next year in between shows on tour. I couldn't wait until the tour finished in August because that would be too late for a season that officially begins in September. Tatiana Tarasova, who had created my programs for the last few years, was out of the question since there was no way I'd have enough time with her after she'd moved back to Moscow.

One night, while sharing quesadillas and margaritas the size of my head with Marina, I realized the solution sat right across the table from me. Marina should choreograph my new programs! I wanted a person to pull something creative and new out of me. Marina, whose powerful reputation in the skating world could only help me politically, fit the bill artistically as well. I asked her to work with me before the ice in my margarita had time to melt.

As Russians tend to do, she mulled it over for a few days, keeping me on edge before accepting the challenge. And a challenge it would be. Marina had a very different aesthetic from mine: hers was modern dance to my old-school ballet. Beyond that, Marina decided that for the upcoming season she intended to get me to skate like a man. I told her, "Good luck." But she didn't find that very funny.

For the short program, we chose a remix of "Palladio" for me to skate like a chess piece, moving deliberately backward, forward, and sideways. Very strong and assertive. Very manly. But for the long program, I wanted to do something with a hot and sultry Middle Eastern vibe. Marina didn't like that idea at all. It smacked of my old fluffy ways. So she came up with a compromise: I would portray the story of Jesus, a strong male figure who also happened to be Middle Eastern. I wasn't exactly looking for geographical accuracy in my program, but I didn't argue after I heard the mysterious, exotic music she composed with Maxime Rodriguez. Plus, after what I had been through at the Olympics, martyrdom did have a certain resonance.

I quickly realized that working with Marina would be a lot tougher than dining or shopping with her. We found some private ice time on our tour stop in Kansas City for our first day of working on the long Jesus program. By now it had been a few months since I had really pushed myself on the ice (not to mention drinking and eating like a civilian). On the ice, I felt like a waddling penguin. Marina only exacerbated my frustration level. Every single time I started a movement—any movement, from lifting my chin to doing a triple axel—she almost immediately yelled at me to stop. Whether it was in French, Russian, or English, she made herself clear.

"No more swan, Johnny. No more swan!"

"You have to be masculine."

"Be a power player!"

"No pretty fingers!"

In that moment I wished I really was Jesus and could send a lightning bolt to torch Marina. No matter what I did, I couldn't skate in a way that she liked. In fact, I could hardly skate at all since she spent most of the time screaming at me to stop. I knew she was trying to get the best out of me, but doing a complete aesthetic overhaul of an established athlete is no easy feat. Marina wanted me to be raw, but for me pretty is my comfort zone. I hated practicing a style that I didn't do well.

Marina's quest for me to man up didn't end at my skating style. She also insisted that my costumes be masculine as well—black and white for the chess piece and brown for Jesus. *Brown? Yuck.* I wasn't allowed to wear even one rhinestone. God was definitely testing me.

By August, it had been a very, very long tour, one that proved hard on everyone's moods and livers. It was also hard on my relationship with Alex, which had been deteriorating for a while. Because we hardly got the chance to see each other in person, we weren't able to solve problems or light that essential spark. Ours had become a phone relationship, and that's never good. When we talked, we were either in a deep depression or angry, the classic poles of the long-distance love affair.

I wanted so badly to make it work that right after the Olympics I talked with Alex about moving to New England. As naive as it might seem now, I wanted our relationship to be one that would last forever and ever, like many do with their first loves. I thought perhaps a change of scenery might just be the necessary ingredient, not only for Alex and me, but also for my skating career. Hoping to marry my professional and personal life, I looked for apartments and had a meeting with Alex's coach right before the tour began.

Alex was really into the idea of me moving. My never being around because of competitions, publicity events, and now the endless tour certainly had put a huge strain on our relationship. But there were issues other than our happiness to factor into the equation. Living in Alex's area would have been expensive and meant I couldn't help out my family financially at a time when my father was dealing with work-related disability issues. In addition, Alex's coach just wasn't good enough for my level of competition.

When the tour hit Colorado I knew I needed to tell Alex the truth: I wasn't moving to be with him. It wasn't a commitment thing. I knew that if I moved up there, we would have become stronger and better—and I wanted that just as much, if not more, than he did. But I couldn't put my family or career in jeopardy. As much as I loved Alex, the Weirs and skating came first and always would.

"I'm sorry, Alex," I said on the cell phone. "You know my family's situation. I can't move. I just can't financially do it."

He was pretty short with me about it.

"Okay," he said, and then moved on to other things.

Alex folded his WASP wings around himself in avoidance, and while I usually agitated for a confrontation, I wasn't going to make an issue out of a disappointment on my part.

Rolling into San Francisco, about a week before the blessed end of this road trip, my castmates and I sat glumly in the silent bus, looking out the windows like inmates about to be dropped off at prison. I was homesick as well as upset from my overwrought work with Marina on the Jesus program. Plus I hated California. It was all bad. Even drinking and eating had lost their allure.

The only thing good about San Francisco, as far as I was concerned, was the shopping. Marina and I put aside our skating differences and made big plans to get matching Chanel bags and be very cute. That was a goal I could get behind. If the tour had been hell, the money was heaven. My car was paid off and I didn't really have any bills, aside from my parents' to pay for, so I felt a little luxury was in order.

Around five o'clock the day of our big shopping spree, we sat down for a bite at a little sushi place, happy with our many purchases and ready for silky fish and soothing sake. Pouring some of the fiery liquid into my little cup, Marina started to talk about the plan for after the tour. We had the skeletons of my programs and now just needed to polish them before the season began in less than a month. The thought of it made my stomach turn.

The waiter placed a couple pieces of yellowtail sushi in front of me when my phone began to vibrate. It was Alex. Immediately, I knew something was wrong. We had a nighttime calls schedule and he was calling two hours early. I left my fish and Marina at the table to answer his call outside the restaurant.

"Hi."

"Hi."

We started to have a normal conversation but not in a normal way. It was like we were talking in slow motion. Then he said it: the worst sentence in the English language.

"I think we should take a break."

I'm not a believer in breaks. They are a pit stop on the way to breaking up. So I didn't accept it.

"Well, I don't do breaks, and you know that about me. So you either break up with me now, or we're still together."

Alex never gave into any of my bullshit, and he wasn't about to now while on the verge of a break from me.

"No," he said. "We're taking a break."

"Okay. Well, then, just know that I consider us broken up," I said.

"Okay. We're taking a break," he said.

I hung up on him, furious that he had one-upped me. After waiting a few moments to see if he'd call or text back, which he didn't, I returned to the restaurant, Marina, and my forgotten raw fish. I sat down at the table and started to sob quietly, tears running down my face from behind my sunglasses.

"What's wrong?" Marina asked with motherly concern.

I told her that Alex had broken up with me and her maternal instinct, turned into Russian wrath.

"Alex is not good enough for you anyway," she said, echoing a sentiment shared by all the Russian ladies in my life who think they know the best person for me to marry.

The love of my life was cutting me loose, but I wouldn't get any sympathy from Marina. So I suggested an alternative, that we go to a bar to get very, very drunk. We ended the night in our beautiful hotel, the Clift, sitting in the stark lobby and flirting with everyone that passed through.

"Oh, you're really going to enjoy your stay," I said as I winked at a couple checking in. "The desserts on the room service menu are amazing."

Drunk hospitality was fun while it, and my buzz, lasted. But the next morning, when I didn't get the usual wake-up text from Alex, the realization of the break hit me hard. His absence festered throughout the day, and there were many times I wanted to pick up the phone to scream, yell, beg, or anything else to make a connection. But I held back, thinking if he was going to come back, it would have to be on his terms.

That day of not speaking turned into several more until I found myself in Bakersfield on one of the very last tour dates. By then I was a shell of my former self, and the song "My Way" had become a dirge. Right before my performance, in my full costume and makeup, I stood in the alley behind the building that housed the rink and indulged in my depression. I put "Ghost" by the Indigo Girls on my iPod and let myself feel the full ache of loneliness while men carted in lights and other stage equipment. Bawling like a maimed cow, I lay down on the ground in a tragic tableau of smeared mascara and rhinestones against concrete.

Having been alerted to my predicament by some other skaters, Marina came running out of the building to find me lying in the alley. She picked me up, dusted me off, and brought me back inside. "You need vitamin C," she pronounced, and, stealing several oranges from catering, made me on-the-spot freshly squeezed juice. "Drink it," she said. I downed the juice, cleaned myself up, and did my performance, crying the whole way through the show.

A week later, after the tour was officially over, I was driving to pick Marina up for a practice at my rink with Priscilla when my phone rang. I picked up the phone. *Alex!* I thought. *Let's see what this bastard has to say.*

"How was your week?" I asked.

"Fine. How was your week?"

"It's been busy."

"Well," Alex said, "did you learn anything this week?"

"No. What do you want me to learn?"

I was getting really agitated.

"I'm really sad to hear that you didn't learn anything," he continued. "I learned something . . . I want to break up with you."

That's not at all what I had been expecting him to say. *I'm young. I'm beautiful. I'm successful. I love him. He's never going to find anyone else that loves him the way I do. He'll come to his senses*—the typical thought patterns of the desperate.

"I want to break up with you," he repeated. "You're not the same person you were when we started dating. You don't treat me like you used to."

It was nothing he hadn't said to me before but the finality of his tone left me breathless. We had been together for two and a half years, always faithful and in love, and now it was simply over? His mom loved me, and I loved her. I loved his whole family—Alex's dad had even invited me to his second wedding. Having wanted happily-ever-after, I was at a complete loss for words. "I'm really sorry that it came to this," I said, crying. "I hope I didn't waste your time. Good luck in your life."

Having made Marina and Priscilla wait for an hour and a half while I talked to Alex, I finally found the courage to peel myself off Priscilla's tarmac driveway and gather my girls for practice. Aware of what the last couple of hours had meant to my life and my happiness, Priscilla looked at me with the pity only a mother could have. Meanwhile, Marina had a far different reaction. "I thought this already happened!" she yelled in Russian.

After two hours on the ice, I drove myself home in a cried-out coma, eyes glazed over, lashes sopping wet, a broken heart.

He was the first love of my life, and there's never one like that again. It makes you crazier than any other love you'll ever have. I didn't know what my life would be like after Alex, or if I could ever love someone again. It had been a depressing summer of too much touring, drinking, and burying my head in the sand. Already August, I had to contemplate getting back into the competitive season after my crushing defeat at the Olympics and my wrecked relationship. I had always thought if I wanted something, I could make it happen. But at twenty-one, I was no longer sure what I wanted or was capable of achieving.

11

Growing Pains

Spokane, Washington, was burning with hatred when I arrived for the National Championships in January of 2007. Pastor Fred Phelps and his insane followers from the Westboro Baptist Church had decided to use the skating competition as a peg for an antihomosexual rally. The group—the same one that threatened to protest the funerals of Amish schoolchildren killed in a shooting rampage because they weren't the *right kind* of Christians—brandished signs outside the official hotel that read "Fags Burn in Hell" and screamed even more offensive epithets. For once, the rage wasn't directed at me personally. Even someone as out of touch with reality as Phelps knew competitive skating was filled with gays, no matter what the U.S. Figure Skating Association tried to promote. Still, my mom worried about my safety. "Stay inside," she said. "Make sure you don't go anywhere."

Phelps and his band of traveling haters were the least of my worries. In the event, where I was shooting for my fourth national title in a row, all the press focused on how Evan was finally going to knock me off my throne. It was true that I hadn't been skating well. My disastrous Grand Prix season leading up to the Nationals had been capped off with my withdrawal from the final after injuring myself during the short program (and after embarrassingly trash-talking Evan for withdrawing earlier because of his own injury).

The federation, understandably pissed that both Americans had taken themselves out of the Grand Prix final, had already started their campaign to make Evan the favorite a year before. The big difference going into the Nationals was that the press had finally gotten onboard. It was almost like the peasants were plotting the fall of the queen. I had been the star. And now I wasn't. In the quest for me to go down hard in punishment for my disappointment at the Olympics, the skating press held up my pop culture moments as proof of how unfocused and undeserving I had become. I was no longer portrayed as an athlete but rather a diva who needed to be put in his place—last place.

The nadir of this new trend came right before the Nationals on *Nancy Kerrigan's World of Skating,* a weekly cable television program hosted by the skating star. She had a few analysts discuss the senior men at the National Championships (basically Evan and me) and they ran me into the ground. Mark Lund, the openly gay founder of *International Figure Skating* magazine, led the charge, calling my swan program tantamount to a big flag shouting "I'm Gay!" "I can't wrap my head around how overly out he is without saying he's out," Lund said. "I'm sorry, but I don't think he's a representative of the community I want to be a part of. . . . And who designs these outfits?" Then he went on to praise Evan as having "a classical elegance and masculinity on the ice I think we need to see in male figure skating. I'm saying I don't need to see a prima ballerina on the ice." He had a right to his skating opinion, but for him to go off on my sexuality was unacceptable. By letting him run his mouth like that, Nancy, a huge force in skating, lent his opinions an air of outrageous legitimacy.

I couldn't outskate the negativity following me into the competition. Although I performed a perfect short program, which three years before would have put me ahead of the pack by a mile, Evan beat me by three tenths of a point. We were basically tied going into the long program, but I knew I didn't have a chance in hell of winning, especially since my long program had been my weak point all season. It seemed nobody liked Jesus. First of all, brown looks terrible on the ice. I tried to change the costume a few times, from brown to gray and then with a pseudocorset-rope belt, but nothing could change the fact that people just didn't want to see the Jesus story portrayed on ice. I couldn't really blame them.

Evan added to my inevitable defeat by giving the performance of his life when he landed a quad toe. I had my own quad toe planned, which I two-footed during my long program—just one in a series of jumps that disappointingly popped. Disconnected from the music and my drive to compete, I imploded in humiliating fashion, living up to the predictions by the press.

Not only did I lose to Evan but I placed third behind Ryan Bradley, a skater who should have never beaten me. Third place meant that I would still make it on the World Championship team going to Tokyo that spring, but all I could think about was one more competition to get through before I could finally say good-bye to this hateful season.

Athletes often talk about post-Olympic depression. You have this giant foe that you're trying to go up against for so long, and once it's over, once it's defeated (or it's defeated you), there doesn't seem to be any reason to go on. After that National Championship, I was just so over it. I had faced uncertainty about whether I should continue my skating career in the past. But this time was different. I felt an incredible ennui. Simply put, I had stopped caring. It was the ultimate defeat.

This depression turned everything in and around skating black, spurring me to look for diversions, albeit brief, from the outside. Right after the Nationals, I was asked to walk in a fashion show for Heatherette, a rock 'n' roll line designed by Richie Rich and Traver Rains. This would be my second time walking in one of their shows for Fashion Week (the designers had invited me to walk the previous year after I met them at an event).

The trip to New York would have to be quick since I needed to keep to my training schedule, no matter how lackluster. But I said yes, desperate to get away from home, the rink, and everyone.

Backstage at the Bryant Park tent where the show was held, I was a bundle of nerves. Walking in a fashion show, when there are tons of celebrities in the first row, is one of the most petrifying experiences, especially when you're surrounded by professional, and gorgeous, models. This year, I had been told, I was kicking off the show. I had better look *good*.

When an assistant shoved my outfit at me (everyone's always in a hideous rush at these things), at first I thought it was a joke. In my hands was a white bodysuit with glow sticks hanging off every inch of it. After finally catching and stopping another one of the assistants, she explained that I was walking in a special section of the show, without lights, wearing glow-in-the-dark clothes and leading a glow-in-the-dark dance troupe.

As the renowned makeup artist Kabuki applied neon products to my face that only showed up under black lights, I felt belittled. I thought I was going to strut my stuff in a hot outfit and makeup. Instead, I was Cirque du Soleil.

While not exactly *Men's Vogue* material, it turned out to be very funny. With people flipping behind me, I walked down the runway, shaking my glow sticks and doing my best style poses in complete blackness.

The fashion show was fun but nothing compared to being invited to Elton John's Oscar party a couple of weeks later. Now *this* was a real diversion that started the minute Paris, my date, and I stepped into the first-class section of the plane and started drinking champagne. The A-List treatment continued when we arrived at the Peninsula Beverly Hills Hotel, where we were treated to a gorgeous room, which was also gigantic. Thank God. Butch and Grämz, who had flown themselves out there coach to continue capturing my life, were also staying in it with us. The Johnny Weir documentary was so low budget that Paris and I shared one bed while Butch and Grämz had the other. It was like fancy camp.

My fashion situation didn't go down as smoothly as my accommodations. Dior had agreed to dress me but by the day of the party, no clothes had showed up. I waited as long as I could before making an emergency shopping trip to Barneys, where I picked up a pair of pants to go with my own black velvet Costume National jacket with beaded lapels that I had brought in case of an emergency. With the Weir luck there were often emergencies.

No outfit could have prepared me for the moment I stepped out of the car and into my first real Hollywood event. I hadn't expected that anyone would want me to walk the red carpet or take my picture. It had been a year since the Olympics, my biggest claim to fame, and the carpet was populated with huge stars—basically everyone who wasn't at the Oscars. But all of a sudden I found myself on this mega red carpet facing a wall of about 150 photographers and cameramen.

"Johnny! Johnny! Johnny!" they shouted.

I loved the sensation: the throng calling my name and snapping my picture. As the flashes went off, I tried to channel Tyra Banks and heed her tips on *America's Next Top Model*. I smiled with my eyes and looked up at the camera while keeping my chin down. I think Mama would have been proud.

Once Paris and I walked into the party, we became nobodies enjoying the craziness unfold. We met our host Elton John, who had no idea who I was, and the cast of *Queer as Folk,* who of course did. I had a particularly good time watching Sharon Stone auction off some car for Elton's charity. Cursing and telling dirty jokes, this famous lady was totally uninhibited in front of people, as if she didn't have a care in the world. I liked her style and envied her power.

Running away to L.A. for the weekend was fun, but I still needed to get my act together in terms of my sport. Skating was who I was and I couldn't run away from it, even if it wasn't going well. Being invited to a few parties was no Plan B.

At this point, hard work wasn't enough. If I continued to skate, I needed to work in a different way. And that meant a new coach. If I stayed with Priscilla, just going through the motions, I probably wouldn't make it through another season, let alone another Olympics.

Over the season, my training situation with Priscilla had become stressed. Both of us were locked in a passive-aggressive war of silent wills. During one session, where I was training for my long program, I missed a triple salchow. I used the mistake on such a simple jump to show Priscilla how much I didn't want to be there by throwing myself down on the ice like an overgrown toddler. Instead of getting in my face about it, she stopped talking, slowly gathered her things, and got off the ice. In that moment, and many that followed, she didn't want to train with me, either.

I escalated the war by habitually calling up my rink and asking them to prep the ice forty-five minutes earlier than my scheduled morning session. After the Zamboni cleared and the ice was still soaked, I skated before Priscilla had even showed up. As she arrived for our session, I would be finishing and, to her astonishment, I would just say "bye" and walk out to the sound of her uncomfortable laughter. By the end of the season we were both avoiding each other, a ludicrous relationship for a coach and skater.

I knew how lucky I had been to start out with someone as nurturing and gentle as Priscilla. Most kids with any hope of becoming competitive skaters begin with hard-asses who have coached Olympic champions. A lot of children drop out because these coaches are too tough too fast. I had a great skating childhood that included the babying and pampering all kids should have. But now I needed a business partner—someone to scare me in the rink—not a babysitter.

My mom could see what was happening and, as my greatest confidante and supporter, forced me to face the situation. After some hard talks, she and I decided that by the time the World Championships finished, I should put an offer out to a new coach.

First I had to find that person. I definitely wanted a Russian coach because I liked the way many of them trained their students. The most radical idea that my mom and I discussed was my moving to Moscow in order train with Tatiana Tarasova. I loved and respected what she was able to do with her skaters. Working with her in the summers, I felt alive—and afraid. Other Russians on the list were Tarasova's ex-assistant coach Nikolai Morozov, who now taught in Connecticut, and Oleg Vassiliev, who had Olympic pair champions in Chicago.

What gave me pause with all those coaches was the fact that all of them worked in the Russian style with a stable of great skaters in a team situation, on the ice together. Growing up with one coach to myself, I worried it would be too much of a culture shock to train in a group full-time.

By the time I boarded the plane for Tokyo, I still hadn't made a decision. Tarasova was the clear front-runner. She expressed interest, but we needed to hear how much money it would be and how we might work out the complicated logistics. I had never lived away from home full-time, so for my first experience to be halfway around the world seemed a bit daunting. There were also skating politics to consider. The federation was not going to like me living and training in Russia—something no American had ever done before.

Meanwhile, Priscilla had no idea that I was planning on

switching coaches because we had kept everything very dis-creet—no small feat in the incestuous world of skating. I felt bad about going behind her back because Priscilla had given me so much and had been a part of the family for so long, but I couldn't tell her until I had secured a new coach.

As if purposefully trying to give me a massive guilt trip, Pris-cilla spent the entire time at the World Championships talking to everyone and anyone about my situation and ways to improve me next season. With the zeal of a crusading physician hell-bent on finding a cure for her patient, she grilled judges, fellow coaches, and officials to amass their best advice. My mom, who always roomed with Priscilla to keep costs down, had to do the lion's share of acting. "Priscilla kept me up until two, making a plan of your summer," my mom said to me wearily over Star-bucks.

When we left Japan after the World Championships, I was no closer to finding a new coach. Nothing felt right. Having next season hang like a big question mark over my head was ex-tremely stressful. The only thing I knew for sure was that who-ever took me on had his work cut out. At the Worlds I placed eighth—a total disaster, just like the current state of my skating career.

———

On the plane back from Japan, I got to talking with two other American team members, Melissa Gregory and Denis Petukhov, husband and wife ice dancers who also trained in Delaware. I normally hate conversing on planes, preferring to shut my eyes to the fact that I'm trapped in such close proximity to other people. But on this trip, I needed to escape from my thoughts and though Melissa and Denis weren't great friends, we bonded over our underdog status in the skating world.

Although an American citizen, Denis was born in Russia, which made him and Melissa less desirable than other pairs in the eyes of the U.S. Figure Skating Association. The married skating partners were always top ten in the World Championships but could never seem to rise to the very top of American skating. Thirty thousand feet in the air, we moaned about the role of politics in our sport and marveled at one another's inherent abilities on the ice. Just like when you're a kid making a new friend and you want to instantly start a craft project or open up a business together, so the three of us mused that we should skate together. But as we discussed it, we became more and more excited about making the concept a reality. And we had a perfect venue—an upcoming made-for-TV exhibition near my hometown in Reading, Pennsylvania, in which we were all invited to perform.

It was a shocking idea, the sort concocted on transatlantic flights, and something big-name skaters just didn't do. In general, well-known skaters don't skate in groups because of the worry that someone else might steal their thunder. And nobody ever mixed ice dancing with singles skating, or pairs skating with ice dancing. It was like dogs mating with cats, complete Armageddon. I had already freaked out the skating community with gender bending and was now fully prepared to do it with genre bending.

Before landing, we came up with the story for our program: we would play fallen angels because that's what we felt like. It would be beautiful and light, but tragic and dramatic—like us. "I'm going to skate with my two wives," Denis joked. Why not? I was already in love.

Getting approval to skate this number from the federation turned out to be like pulling teeth without Novocain. The pain was not surprising but incredibly irritating nonetheless. They absolutely didn't want us to skate together. Anything that veers from the traditional path sends them into a huge tizzy.

Their excuse was that they didn't know how to pay us because there was no scale if we skated together. But the truth is they were terrified. Here you had me, deemed publicly unreliable, and a pair of dark-horse ice dancers? Put those three scary things together and I'm sure they conjured up images of an erotic sex number that would make all the elderly folks tuning into the exhibition at home lose their dentures. We had to explain every single detail of the program, which we only had a week and a half to choreograph, and the whole story behind it. We told them how much we would be skating together and how much apart. The whole process took about a million phone calls and came right down to the deadline before we finally received approval, but the three of us were convinced it was worth the effort because the program would be a revelation.

The Marshalls Showcase was to be held twenty minutes from where I grew up. Kids from my elementary school had entered a writing contest to win tickets for the event and so the rink was stacked with fans from my hometown.

Still Melissa, Denis, and I were nervous about what was going to happen on the ice. All the elements were in place. Denis had procured us ethereal music from Globus, a band that does music for many movie and TV trailers, and we all had matching blue and white costumes as light as a cotton candy confection. The choreography expressed the essence of three angels, alone and connecting in loving, chaste, and barely there touches. I added the final drama with crazy blue makeup à la Hamburglar on our faces. But because of the fast turnaround time of the program and the effort that went into getting its approval, we had only one run-through together. It didn't help that backstage, officials and other skaters were staring at us like freaks. Three of us skating together. The horror!

On the ice, while clasping hands before beginning, I could feel Melissa and Denis's sweaty palms. We had more riding on this than just a TV performance. The three of us had become great friends, and as with all my friends I wanted to help them out. In this particular moment that meant getting them a spot on the Champions on Ice tour, which was about to begin. They needed the money and I needed the friends on tour. The only problem was Champions already had a pair of ice dancers. It would be a hard sell to bring on Melissa and Denis, but if this program made the right kind of waves, we had a shot. If it didn't go off perfectly, we would never be allowed to do it again.

I was so used to skating alone—either pissed or ecstatic with myself—but with two other people on the ice I got to be part of a team. Having been so isolated in my sport for so long, I relished the feeling of moving in sync with Melissa and Denis. The audience, even if they didn't understand the groundbreaking aspect of the moment, sensed our excitement and came along with us for the tender ride.

When we finished, the crowd rose to its feet, having received the program in the way we had hoped. The TV commentators, who had expressed wariness when we took our starting positions, offered unadulterated praise. Even the bewildered skating folks backstage slapped us on the back. The number had been an unmitigated success.

But the best attention was the mainstream interest our number garnered the next day on PerezHilton.com. The gossip blogger, who has been a big supporter for a long time because he loves my kind of crazy, found a YouTube video of the program and posted it on his site. The video ended up with upward of one hundred thousand hits over a couple of days, way more than figure skating usually gets, because Perez had exposed our work far beyond the usual scope of those tuning in to the Marshalls Showcase.

Melissa, Denis, and I had bypassed the pettiness of the federation and brought a stunning, personal moment of skating directly to the people. With hard page-view numbers behind us, we made our pitch to perform the program on the Champions on Ice tour. It took some negotiating and a trial period of a couple of show dates (where the directors realized that people bought tickets *just* to see this act), but Melissa and Denis landed the gig. That summer these three fallen angels were loved and accepted everywhere.

———————

While on tour, I spent a lot of time talking to people about ideas for a new coach. It was Viktor Petrenko, a gold medalist in the 1992 Olympics, who first brought up someone nobody had mentioned before: Galina Yakovlevna Zmievskaya, his former coach and current mother-in-law. The idea intrigued me. A lot of the pieces seemed to be in place for a good partnership. Tough and Russian, she didn't have any major men skaters so could offer me personal attention. Galina's rink was only a two-hour ride from Newark, so I would have to move, but not as far as Moscow, which would make my mom happy. Plus, Galina had a great history, having taught my idol Oksana Baiul.

At the first opportunity, my mom and I set out to have a meeting with the great Galina. Of course the Weir family luck struck and we had a disaster getting there. Flooding in Bergen County meant we couldn't cross a certain bridge and had to weave our way through the back roads, getting very lost and arriving really late. Even though I was an Olympic athlete, who garnered a lot of attention in my sport and beyond, I still felt it was incumbent upon me to impress her. That's just the way it is when you work with coaches. Like Marina, who kept me waiting before agreeing to choreograph for me, the power dynamic always seems to spin in their direction. I worried that when we didn't show up on time, she wouldn't honor the meeting.

My fears proved unfounded. In the middle of training her daily crop of kids, she got right off the ice to greet me. A classic Ukrainian babushka with pinkish-blond hair in a red down comforter coat approached us with a formal nod. She didn't say hello or speak any English, preferring instead to have Viktor translate. The hour-long meeting was quite a family affair, with Nina, Viktor's wife and Galina's daughter, also present.

"I don't need a best friend," I said. "I need a jump start in my career."

Still pretty cocky despite my floundering career, I felt I was at a level where any new coach wouldn't really have to teach me, just kick my ass.

But Galina, exuding the air of a businesslike grandma, had devised a plan—and I hadn't even said yes to her.

"Galina already told me that she wants to work with you," Viktor said, "if it's the right fit. It's going to be hard work. There are a lot of things we want to fix. We aren't here to babysit you."

Fix? Priscilla had taught me great technique. I needed discipline but I wasn't sure about fixing.

"I've studied your skating. You're very fun and unique," she said through Viktor. "You have all this raw talent, but you're not using it. And I want you to be able to use it. I want you to have stronger technique on your jumps."

As this little Russian ballbuster rattled off my flaws, at first she made me feel mildly uncomfortable, like a film or TV actress caught outside her home with no makeup on. Then she gained my respect. I didn't think my jumps needed work, but I realized that if she's not afraid to say all these things to my face and offend me, she can probably do great things for me.

"We need to change your image to the skating world," continued Galina, wise words from a woman with years in the sport. "You need people to think you're a serious athlete."

That's what I was changing coaches for, or at least what I thought at the time. I was ready to sign up.

On the drive home, my mother and I hashed out all the details and made our decision: I'd move to New Jersey and be on the ice training with Galina by the first week in August.

The only other person I had to convince was Paris. I had never lived alone before and going through all these changes careerwise, I didn't know if I could go handle it all by myself. Paris would provide a great support system and much-needed comic relief. He also needed a change. There wasn't a lot going on in Delaware for him. He had quit skating and many of our original group of friends had moved away. Having lost his way a bit, he, too, needed to grow up. Paris was onboard, not so much for any of those reasons. He loved the idea of living close to the madness and adventure of New York City.

We headed to New Jersey with my mom for the weekend to look at apartments. When we arrived at one immaculate complex filled with perfectly appointed orchids and pictures of smiling families of all ethnicities enjoying the place's amenities, the man who showed us around turned out to be a fan of mine.

"Hi, Mr. Weir," said the agent, who was obviously a gay man. "Welcome. I've been waiting for you all day. I love your skating."

Paris and my ears perked up right away, sensing we could get something out of this guy. I didn't know what Paris was thinking—probably keys to a secret roof deck. But I was thinking about a job for my new roommate. We couldn't move up here together without him finding a job, or his parents would make him move back to Atlanta. I remembered that in one of the many career paths Paris had pranced down, he had earned a real estate license from Delaware.

After finding a great apartment that Paris and I agreed to take, I batted my lashes at the agent.

"You know, Paris has his real estate license. And he really needs a job," I said while Paris was in the other room, checking to see if the tub had a Jacuzzi feature.

"Have him send in a résumé and I'll see what I can do. He has to be legitimately able to do this job," the agent said with stars in his eyes. "But I don't see a problem with my helping him."

Paris and I practically skipped out of the complex. This crazy scheme for our lives was going to work out after all. Paris turned to me before getting in the car and made a serious face.

"Nicky, you know you're going to have to sleep with him for me to get the job," he teased.

"For you, Paris," I said. "Anything."

Telling Priscilla was going to be even harder than finding Paris gainful employment. But time was running out. I had already been selected for the Grand Prix events in China and Russia, two powerhouse places to compete, and it was getting close to the point in the season where a skater has to decide choreographers, music, costumes, and the rest.

On every break from the tour, she tracked me down.

"Johnny, I need you to come over to the house for a little bit tonight. We have to discuss the plan."

I kept dodging her, finding any and every excuse to get out of a meeting. As the weeks rolled by, her stress level and messages on my voice mail increased.

"I have a very good plan for us."

"Johnny, we need to talk about what we're going to do. Call me back!"

Finally I couldn't procrastinate any longer. I was on the cusp of moving to New Jersey and had to cut ties with Priscilla once and for all. I called her on a random Wednesday morning in the middle of touring with Champions on Ice and said my mom and I would be over that afternoon to talk. I knew that she thought it would be about the upcoming season and didn't disabuse her of the notion. My mother and I had agreed that she would be the one to break the news. "I hired her," my mom said. "It's my job to fire her." I didn't say no. I wasn't sure I would be able to walk through the door without crying, let alone let go of

Priscilla. Although we had an unworkable relationship on the ice by this point, I loved Priscilla like a second mother. She had been with me almost every day since the age of thirteen. This was going to be incredibly sad.

When we arrived at her door, we could see in her clear, open expression that she didn't suspect a thing. No sooner had my mother and I sat down awkwardly on the couch than Priscilla, perched on an adjacent love seat, began going a mile a minute about the upcoming season.

"I read this book . . ."

"I have a list . . ."

"You'll watch this video . . ."

All the ideas she had been so eager to tell me about spilled out of her in a frantic jumble. Perhaps on some level she knew what was coming and wanted to push through it with plans for progress. She seemed as manic as we were uncomfortable. Finally my mom interjected with her typical blunt force.

"Priscilla, it's come to a point where we really need a change. And it's not personal; it's not you; it's not us. It's just, for Johnny to achieve everything he wants to in skating, we have to make a change. He's not improving anymore, and we need somebody that can light a fire under him and make him improve."

"Okay," Priscilla responded, almost like she didn't believe it. "I want you to watch this video before you go."

Completely stone-faced, she stood up and took out a DVD based on the book *The Secret* that she had wanted me to watch in order to wish a medal into reality. As she pressed play, my mother and I shot each other a quick look, like, *What's happening?*

What happened is that Mom, Priscilla, and I spent the next hour watching a video about making our greatest desires happen using ancient mystical secrets by way of various inspirational-speaking palm readers with a dash of psychology and self-help thrown in for good measure. My mom and I didn't know where to go with this. We didn't need to see *The Secret;* we needed to get the hell out of there.

After the movie ended, my mom tried to get us back on the track of firing Priscilla. "We found someplace to go. Johnny is going to leave at the end of the month. And Priscilla, really, this isn't about you. We support you in anything you want to do. Johnny will never have a bad word for you because you guys have had an amazing relationship."

I nodded like a fool because I wasn't going to be able to talk and not cry. Still on her love seat, Priscilla began to slowly comprehend the reality unfolding from my mother's words. "Okay," she said. "Okay."

My mom and I got up from the couch and started to leave. While walking us to the door, Priscilla began crying.

"Priscilla, I would never be what I am, or who I am, without you," I said. "You've been everything to me. You've given me my life. I mean, I can't ever repay you. And I'm so sorry that this had to happen."

My heart was breaking. I knew Priscilla well enough to know that this was the end of our relationship as coach and student, as well as friends. It was like getting a divorce from your parents or having someone die, awful and ugly and sad. I kept telling myself that I had an objective, no matter how much it hurt her or me. I didn't have a lot of time to achieve what I wanted to achieve. *This is the right decision* I said over and over in my head.

"Thank you," I said.

"Just promise me," she said before closing the door. "No matter what, you'll do everything you can to win."

12

From Russia with Love (and an Iron Fist)

"I'm here to see Galina," I said to the teenage boys working the front desk at my new rink in New Jersey.

"Who are you?" one asked.

Oh, lord.

"I'm Johnny Weir. I just moved here to take from Galina."

They looked at me blankly, like they would any other student at the rink. This was not helping my nerves. While driving there I had become more and more anxious. I knew with a judgmental woman like Galina, I would never be able to overcome a bad first impression (I had even practiced the drive over the weekend to make sure I wouldn't get lost and be late). For so long I had been training at the same place with the same people that my routine had become as fixed as stone. Now it crumbled in front of these lanky, pimply boys.

"Well, where do I go?" I asked.

"For what?"

"To change."

"Just go anywhere. Everyone usually sits up in the snack bar."

To change?

"Is there a locker room? I have to get undressed to change."

"You can use the bathroom, I guess."

I was starting to get irritated. Then the woman who owned the rink came around the corner to say she had a key to a locker room for me but added, "Don't tell anyone that you're sitting in a locker room." In Delaware, I could have said, "Will you set off an atomic bomb in my locker room, please?" And they would have done it. But I decided not to freak out, not on my first day at least. "I just need a place to sit that's not a toilet or a snack bar," I said.

I saw Galina on the ice teaching, but I didn't want to interrupt her so I went directly to the locker room to change and stretch. In the musty, cinder-block box, I took solace in the familiar warm-ups and rituals that I had done back in Delaware, tying my skates extra tight and lingering over my hamstring stretches. I got so comfortable that by the time I looked up at the clock, it alarmingly read three minutes past the hour—three minutes late.

With my skates already on, I dashed out of the locker room

and onto the ice. Galina looked at me with a completely straight face—no smile, no hug, no nothing—and I bowed to her as a sign of respect.

"You're late," she said in heavily accented English.

I didn't know where to go with that. With Priscilla, if I had been late three minutes, she would have said nothing and stayed an extra hour.

"Okay, get to work," she said.

I was dying. Three minutes in, I had screwed myself.

Viktor Petrenko and his wife, Nina, were in Russia shooting a TV show, which meant that it was just Galina and I on the ice alone. I started skating around on very stiff legs, doing edges and different footwork passes when she cut me off.

"That's all bullshit; you don't need any of that. We are going to jump right away."

I expected her to be hard on me, but in the first minute? Galina was there to push me, so I did what she said and started jumping. But I had years of experience with warming up for thirty minutes to get my body moving, and *then* jumping. Completely off-kilter, both mentally and physically, I fell all over the place while trying to dodge a group of kids in hockey camp. Galina just stood silently watching me.

"Viktor showed me videos," she said after what seemed like my hundredth tumble. "Your triple axel, everything you do wrong."

Um, maybe something had been lost in translation. People had always revered my triple axel as one of the best in the world because of how fast I rotated, how high I went, and how smooth the ride out and landings were. And she was telling me that I was doing it wrong? I was under the impression that she was here to push me, not change everything about me.

That wasn't even the worst part. Galina speaking in English was kind of like a teakettle about to explode with steam. Whenever she tried to talk, she was bursting at the seams to get the words out. I knew there was so much she wanted to tell me, and she couldn't do it quickly enough. I understood Russian, even if I didn't speak it fluently, but I was too overwhelmed and intimidated to stop the lesson and tell her that.

"Zees jumps vizout contrrrrol," she said, getting more and more frustrated. "Zees teknik. It doesn't vork."

Galina started waving her arms, stopped speaking in mid-sentence, picked up again, stopped—meanwhile I was doing my jumps the only way I knew how as she became angrier. Finally, thank God, she switched into Russian and the details started flowing. She picked apart my jump from the entrance to the landing, breaking it down with a technocrat's precision. She didn't realize at first that she was speaking Russian, but after I followed a few of her uncomfortable commands (falling even harder now) she said, "You can understand me?"

I nodded, already feeling the soreness creep up the mess that would later be my muscles.

"Well, why didn't you tell me that earlier?" she barked.

From the very first day with Galina, I had to change not only my training routine and completely overhaul my technique, but I also had to switch my official language from English to Russian (or at the very least, Englissian). It was a lot to get used to right away—especially considering I was also adjusting to living on my own for the first time.

Saying good-bye to my mother had been a particularly painful part of the transition. While helping me move in a few weeks earlier, she worried about my being alone in a strange place, especially since Paris wouldn't be arriving for several days. When it was time to go, my dad and I walked her out to the jeep while she sobbed. It took everything inside of me not to cry, but I wanted her to have that moment.

That first night, alone in my big bedroom, my courage went right out the window. Even though I was in the most secure building on the safest street, I convinced myself someone was going to come in and kill me and nobody would be around to care or find my body. Terrified, I slept with three knives next to the bed.

But the next day the sun was shining and I quickly found my touchstones—Whole Foods and the Container Store (there are no words for me and the Container Store). I set about stocking the fridge with healthy food and organizing every inch of the apartment.

When Paris arrived not long after, he immediately reversed all my hard work. It was like a tornado descended on the apartment—within minutes he had lost his keys and a $100 bill in the rental truck, put a bag of his clothes in the wrong closet and left a water mark on my new coffee table. He brought all-out madness into my serene new arrangement.

I hadn't been to New York City since I'd arrived, but Paris insisted we leave all his stuff in the car and go right away. So we hopped on a train and in twenty minutes arrived in Penn Station. It was a strange feeling of accomplishment. I mean, anyone can move to northern New Jersey. But there I was on my own, an adult, in the big city. We went directly to Pastis, a French brasserie in the meatpacking district, and had a great meal. It was no accident that the restaurant was right around the corner from one of my favorite stores—Balenciaga. That first day in the city, I bought two of my signature Work Bags in red and green as a welcome gift to myself.

After a few skirmishes with Paris over his housekeeping habits, I acclimated to my new life (the bags helped). But the biggest culture shock by far was working with Galina.

The first few weeks of training together were the most frustrating of my entire skating career. Following Galina's instructions, I no longer could land a single jump consistently. All I did was fall without understanding why. "It's because I'm changing everything," Galina said. "Just be with me. Deal with it. And do what I tell you. You're going to fall for a little bit." She didn't give me the opportunity not to trust her.

Before meeting Galina, I had a very free entrance to my triple axel. Relying on my natural talent, I would kind of wing it and fly into it, which was what made it exciting. But she wanted a very strict pattern for success on the jumps. She wouldn't let me skip a step. First position, second position, third position . . . fall. First position, second position, third position . . . fall.

My body started to scream. With Priscilla, I hadn't jumped that much because I worried about stressing my body. Galina pounded, pounded, pounded the jumps and the footwork and the on-ice running. My ankles swelled up and my body ached in places I didn't even know existed.

As I started to fall apart, the flip side to Galina's harsh task-master emerged in the form of a caring grandmother, who drove me in her white Mercedes to her massage therapist and cooked me chicken cutlets. She brought in weird Russian machines to stimulate my stiff hip and creams that smelled like tires. Galina dove right into the role that she wanted for herself: to control every aspect of my life. If my jumps were wrong, she'd fix them; if I was injured, she had the cure; if I were hungry, she would feed me; if I wanted to go shopping, she would take me.

When Viktor and Nina returned from Russia a few weeks after my first lesson, they were amazed by the bond that had quickly developed between Galina and me. Even more than that, they were startled by the difference they noticed in Galina. I had been so busy falling that I hadn't picked up on it, but Nina and Viktor pointed out that Galina had traded her trademark upscale sweatsuits for proper pants and jackets. She had also lost a little weight and wore her diamonds and best designer bags to the rink every day. I love a dolled-up lady, but, more important, those observations helped me realize Galina was excited about working with me. "She whistles while she's doing her makeup," Nina laughed.

Viktor, who had convinced Galina to take me on, was

thrilled things were working out. I didn't know it at the time, but she had hesitated because of preconceived notions about my personality based on rumors she had heard. Like many others, she expected me to be a diva bitch, crazy and full of myself.

She was also uncomfortable with my being gay. Galina didn't know if she would have to work with me like she would with a woman or a man. Could she yell at me, or would I be really emotional and cry? Her fears were allayed when she understood that not all of us are drama queens like on TV and that I took my falls like a man.

What took Galina longer to adjust to was my celebrity. Not only did I still have a camera crew following me around to shoot my documentary, which she did not approve of at first, but people arrived at the rink wanting interviews and details of how life with Galina was going. In an article published early into our relationship, a reporter described her as a "Bolshevik," which enraged her. How dare they call her that, Galina ranted, she had an American passport. She started to feel the sting of being associated with me.

"Galina, I'm sorry. But with me, people are going to pick you apart," I said. "That's just what we have to deal with. It makes us stronger."

Among the members of Team USA, Galina and I stood out like black sheep—or perhaps more accurately, black Russian bears.

For our first competition, less than a month and a half after we began working together, Galina had told me I needed to wear my American jacket. The event in Shin-Yokohama, Japan, called International Counter Match Figure Skating Competition USA. vs. Japan, was very team oriented. Every team official, such as our president, chairman, and the rest of the U.S. Figure Skating Association's muckety-mucks, were present. She wanted me to make a good impression.

"I don't have one," I told her.

"How come?" she asked, surprised since she had seen me wearing the Russian team uniform to practice many times.

"I shrunk it in the wash."

She shook her head and laughed.

"Please don't wear your Russian uniform, at least."

I listened to her and wore black for the official practice, but the two of us still made quite an impression in the sea of red, white, and blue tracksuits. For the occasion, Galina had decked herself out with a new dye job, diamonds, and big fur coat, despite the fact that it's still warm in Japan in September.

Galina—whose most recent competitive pupils represented countries like Israel, Japan, Ukraine, and Georgia—hadn't been exposed to the U.S. Figure Skating Association for a long time. She had worked with Scott Davis, a high-level U.S. skater, in the late '90s when I'd just started skating, but this was a whole new federation and I was a completely different story than Scott.

From the moment we arrived she didn't speak anything other

than Russian to me because she didn't want the officials and other skaters to understand what we were talking about.

"Put on your Amerikanski smile," she said, the big grin with full teeth that she called the "American smile," part of her campaign to get me to be pleasant and nice around people. Then, in Russian, she asked me to tell her who everyone was and everything about them while they sat directly in front of us. I pointed out the various officials and men and women practicing on the ice.

"That girl looks like a cow. A beautiful American cow," she said.

Galina was so ornery and wonderful. With Priscilla, I could never talk like that because she would get offended. Finally I had found a partner in crime. While everyone watched us, we traded barbs in Russian, treating the whole practice like a performance. The other team members felt uncomfortable with our foreign language and bursts of laughter. "Why are you speaking Russian?" one of the other team members asked. "It's easier for Galina," I lied in my new effort to be a politician.

We had such a great time on that trip, Galina called it our "honeymoon." She immediately snapped onto the fact that I didn't like eating or hanging out with everyone else and loved me for it. "Johnny, I hate going to team parties and eating with the kids," she said. "Let's go have some foie gras." We dined alone on the top floor of the hotel for every meal, feasting on filet mignon and skating gossip.

At the competition, everyone was waiting to see what Galina

had been able to do with me over the summer, and I didn't let her down. The program wasn't perfect—it was still extremely early in the season—but my score was way higher than the other American men. USA won the team competition because of my score.

Afterward a few of the top officials approached Galina with their big Amerikanski smiles. Pleased with the work she had done, they began complimenting her.

"Congratulations," one official said in an unusually loud voice. "He looks like a completely new person."

"A . . . new . . . skater," another said, equally loudly but also very slowly, moving his lips a lot like he was talking to a deaf five-year-old.

Even though Galina had lived in the States for eleven years, they didn't think she spoke English. But they were pleased—we had won because of my placement, after all. They commented that I was prepared (which hadn't always been the case) and skating "much more masculine." I thought it was silly how they assigned a gender category to the orderly way Galina had taught me to jump.

The only thing the federation officials wanted to see were some changes in the footwork sequence to make the program more difficult.

"That's a great idea," she said while smiling and nodding.

Once the federation officials had moved on, she turned to me and said, "Johnnychik, we're not changing anything. They won't know the difference." Galina was not only forming me as an athlete, but also helping with my PR—something I desperately needed. She told them whatever they wanted to hear (something I'm incapable of). Galina, a master at twisting situations to make it seem like she'd do anything to please, turned out to be right. We never altered the footwork sequence that season, but the officials clearly had no idea since they remarked that the program was "so much better."

Sitting in business class on the way home from Japan, we were riding high; it was the Galina and Johnny show. We both had our sunglasses on, and Galina looked particularly fancy in a gorgeous St. John suit ("I only travel in St. John. It's so comfortable," she said). She sipped champagne while I had orange juice since Galina had a strict no-alcohol policy during the competitive season.

The fourteen-hour flight home gave us ample time to talk about our plans for the season. In a month I'd be competing in the Cup of China, as my first Grand Prix event, and then, right after, the Cup of Russia—my red tour. It would be mega competing in Russia because all of Galina's Russian friends, coaches, and skaters would be watching to see what she'd done with this American.

But at that moment there was no pressure, just big hopes and dreams. I felt so good to be part of this great, great love story between the two of us. Galina had brought out the inner gentleman in me. Unfortunately no honeymoon lasts forever.

Going into the Grand Prix season, it was war. First up: China, where I would compete against Evan, who had just defeated me at the U.S. National Championships, and Stéphane Lambiel, a two-time world champion; then directly to Russia, where I faced Stéphane again. Big names right out of the gate was big pressure on both me and Galina. But we held it together as it turned cold in New Jersey. The furs came out and so did our fighting spirit. By the time we boarded the plane to China, we were both prepared—me with hard training, Galina with glowing skin from a facial and all her best things packed.

In China, after skating a clean long program, something I hadn't done in years, I significantly beat my personal best scores. Galina beamed with pride, and I saw my mother up in the stands, waving and crying. Evan skated after me, and it was close. But I won. I'd beat Evan, who placed second, and Stéphane came in third.

Landing in Moscow at the start of November when it gets snowy, cold, and very Russian, I was so excited to be back— proud of what I had just accomplished in China and content to be with a coach whom I adored. Galina, waiting at the airport, had planned a week of fun before we resumed our hard-core training for the competition. We were totally on the same wavelength, amazing for any new relationship.

The fantasy continued when I arrived at my hotel, the Metropol. Located right next to Red Square, it's one of the oldest hotels in Moscow and just a fantastic place to be. Galina hadn't believed me when I told her that I had gotten a great deal on the Internet until she saw my room: a large one boasting antique furniture, a huge chandelier, and a view of the Bolshoi Theatre. Very five-star, but old five-star, so my style.

I woke the next morning feeling like royalty. After training and a massage in the morning, I had lunch with one of my best friends, Russian skater Alexander Uspenski. Then that evening I was set to accompany Galina and her best friend Elena Tchaikovskaya, someone with a lot of history and influence in Russia, to see *Swan Lake* at the Bolshoi. (Elena Tchaikovskaya, Tatiana Tarasova, and Galina Yakovlevna were long considered a troika of the Russian skating world. The grand dames were the best of friends, but Galina and Elena had a particularly close bond and took vacations every May together in the resort city, Sochi.)

At lunch near my hotel, Sasha (as Alexander was known) and I toasted my success in China with a couple of glasses of wine. I knew Galina would have a fit if she found out, but it was only a couple of glasses. Unfortunately that was enough to get me tipsy and make me lose track of time. Our marathon lunch seemed to pass by in minutes.

I raced back to my hotel to shower and change, but Galina, standing outside the Bolshoi in the freezing cold waiting for me, was already calling every two minutes. Just as I was about to exit my hotel and make a beeline for the Bolshoi, I ran into one of my most ardent fan girls. She was hard to miss, with her meticulously applied false eyelashes and giant bust packed into a satin dress. "I want you to escort me to the ballet," she said.

She had somehow found out where I was staying and that I was going to the theater. I wasn't too surprised. In Russia, you can find out anything you want.

"Oh, you're going to the theater, too?" I asked in my wine haze. "Okay, I'll walk you."

I don't know what I was thinking, showing up to meet Galina late, tipsy, and with a girl who looked like a prostitute. Clearly the alcohol had affected me more than I realized because it was the stupidest move ever.

"Get away from him!" Galina shouted at my fan, who instantly scattered in fear. Galina could get really scary.

Then she got up very close to me, peered in my eyes, and sniffed my breath.

"Johnny, you're drunk!"

I wasn't drunk, just a cheap date. Galina let loose with a stream of insults, screaming at the top of her lungs about how disrespectful and shameful I was.

"How Russian can you get?" she said before pushing me inside. "Showing up at the ballet drunk, with a whore."

Luckily all was soon forgiven (even though I slept through half of the performance) and the three of us enjoyed a lavish mini vacation mostly organized by Elena. That week we went to see a stage version of *Yunona I Avos,* which I wasn't drunk for, and watched international skating competitions from the comfort of Elena's grand apartment.

The highlight was dining at a restaurant in Moscow where only famous people are allowed (Tchaikovsky and Pushkin both worked in the dark, quiet place while in town) called Klub Pisateliy. Elena ordered a full Russian feast of *chebureki,* chicken Kiev, piroshki, blini, and, my absolute favorite, black caviar. Although there was a ten-year ban on farming black caviar because of depleted supplies, in Russia certain people can get whatever they want.

When Elena asked for the illegal caviar, the waiter politely said, "Madam, you know we can't give you black caviar."

"I know better," she replied.

The waiter nodded and returned with a huge platter heaped high with black caviar that must have cost a small fortune. I slathered the black gold on one after another lacy blini. God, I love Russia.

That was just the start of the celebration. At the Grand Prix a week later, I skated better than I had in China and won the competition by many points. I made Galina proud . . . for a short while.

After the exhibition skate, I returned to my room to get ready for the skaters' closing banquet, where I was asked to give a thank-you speech on behalf of the athletes in English and Russian. Once I had finished dolling myself up, I went down the hall to Galina's room to pick her up. When she opened the door, I was astonished to find her in a kimono and face mask.

"Aren't you coming?" I asked.

"No. I wasn't invited."

And then she slammed the door in my face.

I was late, of course, and didn't have time to deal with whatever hot flash had caused her to go insane. When I got to the banquet, I asked one of our team leaders why Galina didn't have a ticket. "You didn't pay for one," he said. Uh-oh. I had messed up bad. Because Priscilla had never attended the banquets, I had no idea I was supposed to buy my coach a ticket. I had just assumed the event would provide her with one. I quickly got a ticket and ran back up to Galina's room.

She was still in her kimono when I begged her to come to the banquet: "I'm so sorry for the mix-up. Please throw some clothes on and come with me."

"No, no, no. I'm fine," she said with raised eyebrows, an expression that I would get to know all too well, and closed the door.

I turned back and headed for my celebration, dejected after experiencing my first real taste of Galina's coldness. After three weeks on the road, we were starting to grate on each other. That amount of togetherness would strain any new romance.

I awoke to a searing pain in my neck. My head, neck, and shoulders felt like a single block that didn't belong to the rest of my body. I tried to move my head but couldn't, an alarming discovery less than a week before the National Championships. As I got out of bed, my entire back spasmed, sending wince-inducing shocks through my hips and down to my toes. If this mysterious injury didn't kill me, Galina was certain to.

Although I had a great beginning to the season with my wins in China and Russia, I had failed at the Grand Prix Final in Torino: Evan had beaten me. That made winning at the Nationals my only shot at regaining my supremacy over him. Since returning from defeat in Italy, Galina had been way more taskmaster than grandmother. She was intolerant of any mistake and not too impressed with any success.

I arrived at the rink hoping that my back would miraculously loosen up or that I could fake it through practice. But in order to jump you have to turn your head to see where you're going. From the minute I hobbled on the ice, it was clear to me, and Galina, that I couldn't possibly skate. I had to fess up about my pain.

She started kicking the walls, spitting and screaming.

"What did you do? Are you partying? Are you . . . ? What's going on . . . ?"

"I don't know why. Maybe I did it lifting groceries, or vacuuming."

"Go home," Galina said.

No matter what my chiropractor or masseur tried, neither could work out the spasms or my stiff neck. I took anti-inflammatories and used an electric stimulation machine but my back remained in pain even as I boarded the plane to Saint Paul, Minnesota, where the competition was held.

Nobody knew about my back injury let alone how severe it was. Galina used the electric stimulator on my back right before I went out on the ice, where I fought against the pain and skated perfectly clean. In first place, I beat Evan, who had made a mistake. But our scores were very close, so I knew if the judges could have found any excuse to put him in first they would have.

In the long program, I faced the judges' bias, back pain, and the first quad toe I had attempted since last year's Nationals. Because of my bad back, I hadn't skated a full long program for almost two weeks, which left me worried that I wouldn't make it from beginning to end. To add to the pressure, I was the very last skater in the championships—not only of all the men, but also of the pairs and women. I had to be a showstopper.

I moved past the pain and landed my quad toe. Other than one small mistake on the last one, I landed all my jumps: the triple axel, a triple toe, and another triple axel. Every element fell into place. The crowd jumped to its feet, and I started crying. Galina, who knew how hard I had fought to keep it together, teared up while I bowed to her and Viktor. Comparing the crowd's reaction to Evan to what they were giving me, I sat in the kiss and cry expecting national title number four. Galina gave my hand a little excited squeeze.

My score popped up in the little TV set at our feet—244.77. The number put me in an *exact* tie with Evan.

It was ludicrous, with the new and intricate judging system, to have two people with the exact same score. Getting hit by a meteor in the middle of the rink seemed more likely.

Our scores were tied, but Evan officially won the title because he had beaten me in the long program by a tenth of a point. Even though I was better, and the audience wanted me to win, I still lost.

Afterward there was a shit storm in the media and people protested the results, accusing the judges of fixing it. Gay websites cried gay bashing. *USA Today* did a huge analysis comparing my performance to Evan's and the score breakdown. Johnny's Angels started a petition and flooded the federation with letters. Whatever the conspiracy, people were behind me because I had proven I was serious again and deserved everything I achieved. The fans wanted a fairy-tale ending, but they would never get one. In the days after the Nationals, the federation did nothing. They never made even one comment on the matter.

I was more tired than angry. Immediately after the competition, I had to stick around the rink for the medal ceremony and exhibition skate, so I lay down on a couch backstage and fell dead asleep. I was exhausted from what had been a long year. It wasn't just the typical rigors of training and competing that had worn me down but also my new relationship with Galina. She wasn't exactly low maintenance. I found it hard to always be up and play the quiet, sweet, lovely skater, although that's what I wanted for her—a student upon whom she could rely.

Viktor woke me up, and Galina slapped some makeup on me before ushering me onto the podium where I stood, very unhappily, accepting the silver medal.

While I waited to do my exhibition skate, Viktor, Galina, and I sat around drinking: beers for them, a Coke for me. Not usually an optimist, Galina found the bright side of the situation.

"Johnny, you know, this sucks. But it's good PR. People are

saying that you were clearly better. They think you were wronged," she said. "You're the angel in this situation. And people love an angel."

For the exhibition, I skated to Josh Groban singing "Ave Maria"—it doesn't get more angelic than that. But when I got off the ice, I learned of the latest drama in my battle with Evan to wear the halo. It turned out he had coincidentally planned to skate to "Ave Maria" as well. When he heard my music come over the loudspeaker, he ran directly out of the rink and back to the hotel to get a different costume and piece of music. I guess he was worried he wouldn't measure up.

Oh, this would not do. It wouldn't do at all. My hotel room in Gothenburg, Sweden, home to the 2008 World Championships, was impossibly tiny, and even worse, right next to Galina's.

While I had long ago accepted her controlling everything from my eating to massages, I didn't need her sleeping in the room next to mine, listening to me take showers and watch movies through the wall. When I'm competing, I need some space from everyone, including my coach.

The front desk found me a bigger room, away from both Galina and, as a bonus, the rest of the U.S. skating team on that floor. I was in the process of pulling all my luggage together to move when Galina stormed into my room and demanded to know what I was up to.

"My luggage can't even fit in this room. So I'm moving."

"Johnny, this is a perfect situation. I need you here. I don't need you running around with all of your friends and partying before the competition and losing your energy."

Partying? What friends? Did she even know me?

"You need to be here. You're moving just because I'm next to you."

She wasn't completely wrong, but I didn't feel like getting into it with her.

"I'm moving to a different floor."

Galina slammed the door. "Oh, no, you're not," she said, taking the luggage out of my hands. I had experienced enough of her guilt trips to know I was never going to win a fight with her.

"Fine. Fine. I don't need another room, Galina. I'll stay here," I said, annoyed that going into my first Worlds competition where I really had a chance at a title someone inside my circle was giving me grief.

The next day, after practicing and going to the grocery store, I was relaxing in my room listening to music when Galina pounded on my door.

Storming in with Viktor in tow, she started looking around my tiny room, under the bed, in the wardrobe, in the bathroom, out the window, and on the roof.

"Galina, *what* are you doing?"

"I'm looking for that girl."

"What girl?"

"You know exactly which girl."

"I have no idea what you are talking about."

"The girl from the ballet."

"One of my fans?"

Galina had seen the same Russian fan I had appeared with at the Bolshoi walking through the lobby while I was having my wild moment buying bottled water and Ricola at the store.

"Yes, your prostitute."

I was going to have to explain to Galina that gay didn't just mean a love of fashion.

Viktor sat down on the bed and told me to sit beside him.

"Johnny, what are you doing?" he said. "You're completely ruining your chances at doing well in this competition. You're aggravating Galina. She doesn't need this. She's an old woman. She doesn't need this on her heart."

Meanwhile, Galina was repeating from the other side of the room, "Who's here? Who's here? I know somebody's in this room with you."

The insane scene was like something out of a bad Russian soap opera. Finally I looked at both of them and said, "Get the fuck out of my room.

"There's been no one in my room aside from you right now," I said. "And you're doing more to me right now than anyone could ever do. I will see you at the practice. Now get out."

Galina left with fire in her eyes and Viktor walking slowly and methodically behind her.

I tried to listen to music and do my makeup, but I couldn't

relax. The two of them were literally making me crazy. I thought they knew me and that the rumors about my wild reputation were completely unfounded. My problems with competing had to do with psychology, not parties.

By the time I got to practice that night, I was livid. Galina, Viktor, and Nina acted jovial because all the media had showed up, but I don't play games. I'm not about to fake it for anyone. So I didn't speak to any of them. While putting on my skates, I became more and more furious, slamming my laces into the holes. For the first time since I had started with Galina, I didn't bow to her before I began.

Back at the hotel after the practice, Galina and I had the unfortunate luck of winding up in the elevator together. She was so angry that she stood close to the doors, with her back to me, jamming the button for our floor over and over as if it would get us there faster.

I really didn't need this. If she wasn't going to stand behind me for this competition, I would have my mother by the boards. Galina had done her job training me, and I was ready. If we parted now, it would be okay.

I knocked on her door.

"Galina, we need to talk."

"Johnny, this all started because you wanted to switch rooms. All the drama is because of you. I don't trust you right now. I don't trust that you have your best interest at heart."

Then she rattled off all these skaters, through the years, who had hung out with their friends through competitions, partying and drinking and losing. Galina listed all the people I had hugged and said hello to, accusing me of inviting them to my room to play and have fun.

"You're going to ruin yourself."

"Galina, I wanted to move rooms to get away from this whole team . . . and you."

"You can do what you want," she said. "But I want you to know that I'm watching, no matter where you are."

The drama was done, but she didn't accept me and I didn't accept her. The tension didn't abate until after I had skated my short program better than I had skated all season and earned a new personal best score. I was in second place, the highest I had ever been in the World Championships. The slate had been wiped clean. Galina, Viktor, and I all hugged as if nothing had happened. Winning will do that to you.

Going into the long program, it was very important I do well, not just for me but also the entire U.S. skating team. The men were closing the Worlds this year, and so far no Americans had won any medals—no women, no pairs, nothing. Our country had done terribly, which was pretty embarrassing since it was a year the federation had spent a lot of extra money creating a program with the specific purpose of winning more medals.

Pride wasn't the only issue. It was important for the following year's World Championships in Los Angeles that the Americans place high enough to secure three starting positions. It would be humiliating if we had bad placement in the Worlds hosted on our home turf. Not only that, but the World Championship in L.A. also decided how many spots the United States would get for the next Olympics.

With Evan having withdrawn from the World Championships a week before because of an injury, I was the top American in Sweden and the last chance for a medal.

In addition to all this drama with Galina and Viktor, there was also this crushing burden to win a medal for my federation, which didn't appreciate me, and, of course, win my first medal for myself.

It's no wonder then that when I got on the ice for the long program, stiff and cottonmouthed, that it went by in a flash. While it wasn't unusual for me to finish a performance and not remember exactly what happened, this time it was literally like a big blank; I had no idea what I had done in the past four minutes.

"Did I do the quad toe?" I asked Galina in the kiss and cry.

"Yes. Two feet on the landing."

"The triple axel?"

"Yes, you did."

My score brought me out of the surreal moment and back to reality: I was in first place with a few more skaters remaining to skate. Before long I learned that I had earned a bronze, not the medal I had hoped for, but still a huge victory. I had earned my first Worlds medal and the only one for the United States. I came through for my country and helped secure three spots for next year's World Championships in Los Angeles. I was ecstatic.

This finally seemed like the fairy-tale ending everyone had been hoping for.

After the euphoria had mellowed, the press conference finished, the drug tests taken, and I made my way back to the hotel, I found myself again knocking on Galina's door. She answered, wearing her kimono. All's well that ends well, but I still needed closure on why she had created so much chaos.

"If we're going to continue to work together, I really need to understand what this was," I said.

"Well, Johnny, when you go to competitions, you always need some kind of drama. Before China, it was trouble with your skate sharpening. Before Russia, you know, we had the fight about you showing up drunk to the ballet. Before the National Championships, you had your back problem." She's like, "Everything was moving along too smoothly on this trip, so I wanted you to be upset. I wanted you to be angry so that you would skate well. I did this for you."

I didn't believe a word of it. She was pissed that I had wanted to change rooms and tried to play it off like she was inspiring my fighting spirit. I found myself aggravated yet again, because I couldn't call her on it. If I had called her a liar, she would have thrown me out the window.

"Congratulations," I said wearing my Amerikanski smile. "We did this together. I'll see you when we get home."

Boarding the plane back to New York, I was extremely grateful the season's end had finally come and that I was traveling alone. Galina had certainly done a lot for me—bringing me back from the brink of disaster to a World medal—but we needed a little break from each other.

Just as I had settled into my seat, closed my eyes, and prepared for a relaxing, silent trip, one of the flight's crew got on the PA system. "Ladies and gentleman," he said. "We would like to announce that our new World Championships bronze medalist Johnny Weir is on the flight with us." Everyone onboard started clapping. Fairy-tale endings might be something I could get used to.

13

Weircapades

Waking up alone in a Korean hotel on Christmas Day was just sad. Even though I'm not one to really celebrate holidays (not only does my tightly structured life not allow me time to enjoy them, but I'm also not a big believer in enforced fun), this was a little too *Lost in Translation* even for me.

But I couldn't say no to the amazing, charity gig where I'd be performing in a Christmas show with the country's top champion Kim Yu-Na. So four days after I competed in the 2008 Grand Prix finals in Seoul, I was back at JFK to return in what would be my twelfth flight to Asia that year.

Another Grand Prix season had flown by in a whirlwind of

travel, training, and, alas, unlike the previous one, defeat. The year started out on the wrong foot when I discovered that my blades weren't aligned properly on the new skates I had received at the end of the summer. It felt like I was walking on a stiletto with one foot and a ballet flat with the other. Not comfortable. On the ice, I couldn't stand straight and had a lot of problems with my jumps. But it was too late to get new boots because the process of breaking them in to a point where a skater can jump safely takes time. I just had to make the best of my stiletto-ballet combo.

At my first event, Skate America, a competition I had avoided until this point in my career because of the early date and the bias against me in my own country, Evan and I lost to an unknown Japanese skater. Evan placed third, and I second, which was humiliating for both of us in our own country. The only highlight was seeing Evan, who had gone to Tarasova for help with his programs that year, come out in a crazy costume that made him look like a waiter. The sparkly penguin suit signaled to me that Tarasova, who had always promoted my skating over Evan's in her TV commentary, was messing with him.

Then I came down with bronchitis for my second event in Japan. With an army of my Japanese fans in tow to help her translate, Galina mined the pharmacy for every remedy allowed under the international skating regulations. With death warming me over, I competed and miraculously placed second. But there were no more miracles left by the Grand Prix final in Seoul. After two solid weeks of fighting with Galina, feeling sick, and skating on my wonky blades, I had no more fight left. I fell in the short program and placed third.

It was a tribute to my Asian fans, whose love didn't waver with my uneven scores, that I was the only non-Korean invited to perform in this huge Christmas spectacular. So although I was wrung dry by the last couple of months, I still felt proud to be there (plus, I loved the star treatment they lavished on me from the minute I stepped off the plane).

On Christmas, the day of the show, I didn't have too long to experience the holiday blues because my new manager, Tara Modlin, landed in my hotel room like a hurricane. I had changed from my previous manager at Michael Collins Enterprises—one of two big skating agencies—after Tara wooed my mom and me over a cozy meal at Elmo. A former skater, she understood my world but was young and new to the business. I wasn't worried. By that point a homeless person could have done a better job than my manager, who would literally take two months to return my call. My previous manager even went as far as to go on Nancy Kerrigan's TV show (only a year after I had been publicly humiliated on it when Mark Lund made rude comments about my skating and sexuality) to say, "Johnny will do better this year because he hasn't been partying as much." With the Olympics looming, I wanted a go-getter and Tara fit the bill. She's a very forceful girl who loves cowboy boots, rhinestones, ruffles, sparkles, and polka dots. She's also very clever and gets what she wants.

Although Tara had been my agent for only a few months,

this was our first real experience together, because at competitions Galina didn't like her talking business anywhere near me.

After quickly washing her blond bangs in the sink, Tara escorted me to the rink for the show. On the way there, I started to feel a little queasy but I made a joke of it, teasing Tara that her perfume was making me sick. But after the rehearsal, where I learned the opening number, I was no longer joking around; something was terribly wrong with me. I felt like a narcoleptic because I couldn't keep my eyes open. When the shaking began, I lay down in front of a heater. Then the puking started. I couldn't stand up straight without puking. I couldn't lie down without puking.

With only three hours before showtime and me puking nonstop into a box that Tara held like a champ, a team of doctors ran in to cure me, or at least get me through the next three hours. Their medicine was as foreign to me as their country. One doctor tried to bleed the illness out of me by pricking all my fingers, while an acupuncturist put needles in my stomach and head.

Everyone needed me to get on that ice, most of all me. It was big, big money, and if I didn't perform I would have traveled to Korea, missed Christmas with my family, pissed off my mom, and become sick for nothing. I told myself that I would skate, even if I had to puke into a sparkly glove during the show.

While lying on a massage table in a parka and under fourteen blankets, I asked Tara to pull the mirror over to me. With only one eye open at a time, I started putting my makeup on my stone-white face. Then Tara took my pants and top off like she was changing a baby and helped me into my costume. Five minutes before my number, three Korean doctors carried me to the ice with Tara holding a giant box in which for me to get sick. With no warm-up, no nothing, I threw up in the box, got on the ice and skated to the center.

Somehow, I skated both my numbers without throwing up or fainting, although I could sense fear in Yu-Na's eyes as she took my hand in our pairs performance.

As soon as I finished, I skated right for the back door, where I puked three times into my box before an ambulance picked me up. The paparazzi waiting outside took photos of me swaddled in coats and blankets like a big baby. People in the hospital also took pictures of me as they wheeled me to a private room.

After weighing me and discovering that I had lost eight pounds in one day, they wanted to hook me up to an IV immediately. Suffering from dehydration and exhaustion, I was sicker than I had ever been in my life. I wanted to feel better, but it's terrifying for an athlete to be in a situation like this where you have no idea what they are putting into you. We had to find a doctor who could translate from Korean into English, and then call an American doctor before they put any needles in me. It was the middle of the night on Christmas Eve back in the States, so it would have to be a Jewish doctor—Tara found one in five minutes flat.

A much harder task was calling my mother. "Patti, everything is okay," Tara said in her sweetest voice. "Don't freak out. We're in the hospital but it's under control."

Of course my mother freaked out and burst into tears.

"He just has exhaustion," Tara explained. "He threw up his entire life today, but he'll be fine."

By now Galina was used to me crying since I had done it just about every day at practice since returning from Korea. The National Championships were only two weeks away, and I still hadn't been able to regain the strength I had lost from my illness over the holidays. Galina yelled at me out of frustration, reminding me over and over that she had warned me not to go to Korea. Still, I would sleep through morning practices out of sheer exhaustion. The weight I had lost during my illness had taken my already thin frame into concentration camp territory. I had no energy and now no jumps.

It was a terrifying moment when my jumps left me. Stuff that I could do since I was thirteen vanished. It's not uncommon for skaters to wake up one day and find they've lost technique, but it had never happened to me. Going into my triple axel, all of a sudden I didn't know what to do and landed flat on my back where I stayed, crying, of course.

This year's Nationals was an even bigger deal than usual because it decided the U.S. skaters that would go to the upcoming World Championships, held in our backyard. No matter how international I felt or how many of my fans came from abroad, I wanted to compete against the world on American soil.

All I wanted to do was make the World Championship team whatever way I had to do it. But it was going to be tricky. Going into the Nationals, I knew there was no way I would do well. I was a total mess. And the U.S. Figure Skating Association, unlike most other countries, based their world team almost strictly on placement at the Nationals. Even if I was third, I'd be fine with it. I just wanted to be on that team.

Once we arrived for the event in Cleveland, Ohio (where I'd had my disaster in the National Championships as a junior-level skater), Galina forbade me from telling anyone—media, fellow skaters, and, God forbid, officials—about my sickness. This wasn't a new policy. She had always been very strict about not discussing illnesses or injuries. "Nobody's going to care. It doesn't matter if you're sick, if your mom just died, if your leg is falling off," she said. "If you show up and you're planning to compete, you compete. Nobody cares about the backstory."

So I went in for my short program looking inexplicably shaky, white, and as emaciated as a heroin addict. I wish I *had* been on drugs after the performance I gave. Although Galina and I had worked back from the basics to rebuild the jumps I had lost, instead of a planned triple axel, I only did a single axel, among many other minor mistakes, all of which landed me in seventh place. I had never been lower than sixth place in a senior National Championship, and that was at my very first.

People were bewildered. Conspiracy theories for my terrible condition abounded: I had a drinking problem; I was on drugs; I was having orgies.

I screwed up the network programming—television had to air the event for the long program earlier because I was no longer in the last group of the top six competitors. When I took to the ice for my long program, many of the audience hadn't yet filed into the building. I was skating to crickets.

With my thin frame barely holding up my costume, I began by popping another triple axel into a single. Then all ninety pounds of me started to fight back. I did the second triple axel followed by a difficult combination. I poured every last bit of strength that I had onto the ice and felt a small seed of hope bloom from my exhaustion. I went up for the last jump and then, *bam,* I fell on my face.

Even though my condition was beyond terrible, I was in total disbelief that I hadn't pulled it together. My scores went up, pronouncing a very bad fate: I got fifth. "I can't believe you let this happen to yourself," Galina said under her breath while smiling for the cameras and crowd.

Immediately after the event, Galina ran into the hallway to start campaigning on my behalf, finding out who was in charge and what we had to say to get a spot on the World team. I was close enough to the top three that the committee could conceivably do something to get me to the World Championships.

In first place was Jeremy Abbott, who was legitimately the best and deserved to go. Evan, a clear champion, was third and should also go. But the second place spot had gone to a skater fresh off the junior level who'd had that wow moment. He had won the silver medal in the Nationals fair and square but most likely wasn't ready for a huge international event, especially one that determined the number of skaters that the United States would be able to send on its men's roster to the 2010 Olympic Games. The problem was the committee couldn't justify replacing a boy in second with me and keeping Evan, who was in third.

The selection committee went behind closed doors right after the event to hash out the possibilities. A few people wanted to see the junior boy go to the Junior World Championships and learn to compete internationally before heading to the big leagues. But it would be especially painful if he got trounced the year the competition was held in the United States. I still had a chance.

Finally, after a torturously long time, a little old woman shuffled out of the meeting room and taped a small piece of paper to the wall, right under our event results. I was named the second alternate for the World Championships, not even the first alternate. That was the end of my season.

I was the only American skater in any discipline to win a world medal the previous season, and the reason that the United States could send three men to the World Championships in the first place, but none of it counted. I had no money in the bank as far as the federation was concerned. I had lost fair and square, by their count, and didn't deserve a spot on the team.

All I wanted to do now that my fate had been sealed was return to my hotel room and kill myself. But I still couldn't leave. In a cruelly ironic twist, I had won the *USFSA's Skating* magazine's Reader's Choice for favorite skater of the year and had to stick around to accept the award. The timing couldn't have been worse. It seemed the federation thought so, too, because minutes before I took the podium with my prepared speech they had asked me earlier that month to give, someone let me know there would be no speech.

I was glad that they didn't give me the opportunity to speak, because nothing pretty would have come out of my mouth. Wearing a USA jacket that I borrowed from somebody else (another stipulation for getting onstage), I accepted the award, waved at the audience, got off the stage, then threw the jacket onto the floor and walked across it.

Back at the hotel, everyone was gathered in the lobby bar celebrating the end of the event and the season. Skaters, coaches, parents of skaters, they were all drinking and having a merry time. That is, until I walked through the door. Every single person's head turning to look at me made a collective whooshing sound. Then the place went silent in wait for my reaction.

I made a beeline for my mom, who was sitting with Tara, my grandmother, and my aunt Diane. Everyone was crestfallen and drinking, even my grandma. I went to my mother, puffy-eyed and drinking Southern Comfort, and hugged her. Sometimes, as an athlete in a solitary sport like skating, it's hard to realize there are all these people who want you to succeed as much, if not more than, you do.

"I'm so sorry," my mother said.

It was too much for me to take. I could barely contain my

disappointment, let alone that of my family and friends. I rushed out of that scene, past the gossiping skating mothers and my fans from Japan crying in the lobby.

In my room, I called down to room service and ordered three orders of chicken fingers and french fries with a soup bowl full of ranch dressing. After it arrived, I locked the door and ate every last chicken finger and left only a random scattering of fries, crying the whole way through my meal.

Then I called room service again and ordered some cake. I was having a major depressed-girl eating situation. A Russian woman, who worked in the kitchen and knew what had happened to me, sent an assortment: a giant piece of chocolate cake, apple cake, pie, and tiramisu. My spies are everywhere.

I vowed right then and there that I would never do a thing to please anyone in that federation ever again. While I had never conformed to their ideal image, I had also never gone against them in any major way. Through all the years of gossip and judgments about me, I always felt the federation supported me in the most important way—by sending me to competitions. But after the debacle of last year's tie at the Nationals, their decision to keep me off the World team felt like an unbearable stab in the back. I would never again wear the American jacket. Not because I don't love and support my country, but I refused to wear anything that had to do with the United States Figure Skating Association.

The grudge between me and my federation was permanent, and mutual. By the next Nationals in 2010, we were in a full-on war.

I was really angry going into the Grand Prix season. After Evan, my chief rival, had won the World Championships, I couldn't help but wonder what would have happened if I had been able to compete. As a gold world medalist, Evan was now the definitive reigning angel.

Russia and Japan, my countries, had picked me for their Grand Prix events. When I got to my first event in Russia, it had been more than nine months since I had set foot in a competitive environment. The time away showed and I placed fourth. In Japan I redeemed myself, placing second before going on to the final, also held in Japan, where I placed third. Although Evan was in first, my place on the podium at least proved I was an Olympic contender.

The whole season was sped up for the Olympics, so the Nationals came on the heels of the Grand Prix final, just after the new year. Back in good old Spokane, Washington, for the event, I knew that I would have to do well here to go to the Olympics. The big question was whether the federation would *let* me do well enough.

At least this time I wasn't at death's door. As with most of the Grand Prix season, my short program went off without a hitch at the Nationals. Evan was ahead of me, and then Jeremy Abbott, who skated shortly after, also jumped ahead of me by a few points. Because he had skated the exact same elements as I had, it seemed like there was some clever judging going on. It had been a consistent theme in my season that my best was never good enough.

Galina and I studied the score sheets as soon as an official posted them. The technical scores were unarguable, but the artistic ones were subjective. That's where the "judging" came in. Among the numbers that were typical for a top-level athlete like myself (the range is normally between 7.0 and 9.0), I saw a few 6's and then one number that made my eyes pop: a 3.75.

"Galina, what is that?" I said.

"Maybe it's a misprint. It should be eight seven five. Eight and three can look like alike," she said.

"I don't think so."

Galina marched up to one of the officials, demanding to know what had happened. A score that low wasn't just bad for me, it was bad for the entire U.S. skating team. It sends a message to the rest of the skating world that one of America's Olympic team is no better than a 3.75—unless they weren't planning on sending me to the games.

Although the identities of the judges are supposed to be kept from their scores for obvious reasons, the official assured us, "We know which judge it is. And we're going to talk to him."

After what had happened at Nationals the year before, I had tried to stop caring about what anyone thought of me. I just wanted to show off what I slaved over every day of my life to the best of my abilities. But it was hard not to care. This sport was all about judgment. Those numbers determined my future.

After the bitterness of receiving a 3.75, I didn't exactly soar into my long program. I skated and did okay, nothing spectacular. Knowing I had no chance of winning, I skated to get the job of going to the Olympics done. It wasn't a conscious decision, but an inevitable one.

By the end of the competition, I was in third place, exactly where the federation wanted me. As I accepted my bronze medal, I became more and more incensed. While waiting for the ceremony, I heard that they were never going to leave me off the team because of my popularity and ability to get a mass audience to watch skating.

After finally finishing the documentary about my life, Butch and Grämz premiered *Pop Star on Ice* that summer at festivals around the country. It was such a success that the Sundance Channel bought it and launched a multi-episode series, *Be Good Johnny Weir,* using the documentary as the first episode. A skater with a reality show on cable, I was a complete anomaly. As if to highlight that truth, Sundance aired the series' promo during the Nationals that showed me in heels jumping out of a giant Fabergé egg. As I said, an anomaly.

Apparently that helped me get an Olympic spot—otherwise they would have sent Ryan Bradley, who placed fourth, ahead of me. I was going to my second Olympics, not as a world-class competitor, but as a trained monkey to sell tickets. I was a token, and there's no worse feeling.

If the federation wanted attention for skating leading up to the Olympics—well, I got it for them. But perhaps not in exactly the fashion they had hoped.

It started immediately after the Nationals with my exhibition skate to Lady Gaga's "Poker Face." The genesis of the program—as far as I could go from the typical Disneyesque fare offered by my sport without getting censored on network TV—was a Fashion Week event the year before. *V Man* magazine had asked me to skate to Beyoncé's "Single Ladies (Put a Ring on It)" at a party celebrating the end of Fashion Week. Beyoncé was so not my style, so I suggested something by Lady Gaga.

Ever since she hit the scene, I have been a fan of La Gaga. Although she's obviously got an obscure vision, she's a real artist. I love her music but am most inspired by the fact she clearly doesn't give a shit about what anyone thinks. Gaga will wear a big old lobster on her head or a dress made out of Coke cans if that's what she wants. Anyone that conforms bores me, and anyone who doesn't has my complete admiration.

The fashionistas at the party held at Manhattan's Chelsea Piers loved the "Poker Face" number, and Perez Hilton put it up on his website where it came to the attention of the Lady herself. She invited me to her concert at Radio City Music Hall, where I sat next to her mother. Mama Gaga, a fan of figure skating, and I got along very well (in general, mothers love me). Dressed in a cashmere twin set and pearl necklace, she stood making the sign of the horns with her hand, sticking out her tongue, and screaming like crazy while her daughter humped a piano bench onstage.

It was a wonderful family portrait. That's how I'd like to think of my mom watching me skate.

True to the spirit of Lady Gaga and her very sexual song, my exhibition number was also very suggestive. Wearing makeup that resembled disco-style war paint and a black, slightly sado-masochistic, corseted costume, I was really excessive for a figure skating show on NBC during a Sunday afternoon. No surprise, a big hoopla followed immediately because even though the program itself was a year old, for the majority of Americans it was their first taste of Johnny Weir since the last Olympics four years ago. Of course it was everywhere in the skating press, but all the entertainment shows featured it as well. People went crazy over watching this silly faggot in makeup, shaking his ass on the ice for TV.

"Poker Face" amplified everything. I mean, it drove people insane. Those who loved me loved it, and those who hated me hated even more. My dirty, sexy dance also made my sexuality a hot topic of conversation. Again.

All the gay websites brought up the question of whether or not I was gay—or, rather, they knew I was gay but couldn't figure out why I was such a jerk that I wouldn't talk about it. This was nothing new. I had been dealing with questions surrounding my sexuality since I was sixteen, when skating fanatics began bringing up the issue on message boards. But now, like my persona, the desire to know who I liked to do it with had grown a hell of a lot bigger. A lot of the gays got downright angry about my silence.

In my career, the gays from an older generation had always been some of my biggest detractors because I refused to perform in the dog and pony show of the traditional coming-out story. When *The Advocate,* a national gay magazine, offered me a cover story after the 2006 Olympics if I came out in the article, I declined. There was no way I would seek publicity with an article focusing on my being gay when that is the smallest part of what makes me me.

Many of those who had to fight for their rights to a gay life think I'm disrespectful because I haven't been out and proud. I'm the first to say it takes enormous cojones to fight to change the world, but not everyone can be an activist. I could never be one; I'm way too passive-aggressive.

Pressure is the last thing that would make me want to "join" a community. I don't appreciate when others push anything on me. I had to fight my entire career in skating to be an individual and not play a role that I was told to, so I wasn't about to step into the chorus line just because the gay community told me to. Yes, I have some very stereotypical gay traits (I love flowers, smelling good, fashion, and I'm an ice skater, for Christ's sake). But I also have traits stereotypical of a Jewish mother (I'll feed anyone I can get my hands on and have a wicked way with guilt) and a regular ol' rural male (I'm not afraid to get my hands dirty and chicken fingers are my favorite food). Being gay is not a choice. I was born gay just as I was born white and male. I don't hold pride parades for the color of my skin or the fact that I have a penis, so why would I do it because I was born a gay man?

Putting people in boxes—whether the label is lesbian, gay, nerd, or freak—is just phony. In our society, too many people box up their personalities, stowing away aspects of themselves that don't fit in the confining shape. In that sense, I wish people would come out, to live freely and openly. I wear my heart on my sleeve. Whether it's with my mother, best friend, or lover, I give everything that I am. To me, gay and straight is only sex. Love is completely without boundaries. The pressure on me to come out was silly because I don't ever remember being in.

So the massive backlash against me in the gay media and community before the Olympics didn't hurt me; it only made me dig my "closeted" heels in further. There were so many articles about my glaring flamboyance that Paris and I talked about how it would be the least shocking thing in the world if I did come out. Apparently everyone in the universe already knew I was a huge flamer. And as someone who's gone far by being controversial in a beige world, the last thing I ever want is to be obvious.

"I should come out as a Pacific Islander," I said. "That would be really shocking."

"No, you should come out as a black woman," Paris said.

"A sumo wrestler."

"Lupus sufferer!"

"French maid."

My true coming-out tale became a running joke between Paris and me, but our fantasies turned out to be far less absurd than the reality of my biggest pre-Olympics scandal. The one that eclipsed my un–family friendly performance after the Nationals and my mysterious sex life, sprung from the tiniest, most mundane detail imaginable.

It all began when I added a patch of real fox fur to one shoulder of my costume because I thought it looked stunning. Anyone who knows me knows I love fur. I think it's glamorous and love the way it feels. I make no apologies for it.

Like me, fur is one of those hot-button issues that stirs up love or hate in people. And the haters are particularly vicious, which I discovered immediately after giving an interview where I talked about the fur detail on my costume. Almost the instant the item posted on the Internet, Tara and Stephanie, my costume designer, were inundated with angry calls. I received hundreds of emails on Facebook about how much I sucked.

Then it started to get really out of control. There were people threatening to obstruct my Olympic performance by showing up in Vancouver to throw blood on the ice while I skated. Someone faxed Tara a death threat and said my head was worth a few million dollars (I was more upset about the paltry bounty than the threat), so she called the FBI. Police were stationed at my rink and circled my apartment complex: a few followed me everywhere in the lead-up to the Olympics.

Although the fur fiasco story had been reported everywhere from CNN to Perez Hilton, Galina hadn't heard about it because she pretty much only consumed Russian media. And I didn't involve her in these kinds of problems because it wasn't part of her job description. She's my coach; she teaches me ice skating and drives me crazy and that's it.

A couple of weeks before the Olympics, she called me on a Saturday afternoon.

"Johnnychik, what's happening?"

"Galina, what do you mean?"

"I just heard on Russian radio that you are in trouble because of the fox."

"Yes, Galina. But I didn't want to bother you with that."

"But why? It's fun!"

"Well, I got death threats."

"Oksana Baiul once got a letter that had actual shit smeared on it because somebody from Ukraine didn't like Oksana, or her mother, rest her soul."

"That's disgusting."

"Don't worry, Johnny. No one's going to kill you. But I still think you should take the fur off."

"Why?"

"Stephanie picked the fur out of some trash bin at a fabric store," she said. "Johnny, that fox is very bad quality. It's a fox that's been dead thirty, forty years."

14

The Last Stand

When I walked into the church late at night, the air felt as thick as honey. The interior's only light source stemmed from dozens of yellow wax candles, which added mystery and emotion in their reflections off the walls' stunningly intricate gold details. There was a weight to this place where so many supplicants had come before, just like me, asking for divine intervention.

I had arrived in the beautiful Russian Orthodox church four days before leaving for the Olympics to receive a blessing after Galina had gotten the idea into her head while watching the Russian Olympic team on TV get similarly blessed by the

Russian Orthodox patriarch in Red Square. In our own corner of New Jersey, she had heckled the local priest (and probably greased a few palms) into giving me a special ceremony reserved for more typically members of the armed forces than athletes.

With the majority of our training team behind me, I stood motionless at the front of the church. In the dark, hushed place, the priest intoned a long series of prayers on our behalf in an esoteric language similar to Russian. Clad in a long ominous black robe, he placed a solid twenty-four-karat gold-covered Bible on my forehead. The coolness of the precious metal sent shivers down my spine as if to jolt me into the rarity of the moment. Then he shook holy water over me, and I felt the emotional magic, a brilliant cleanse of spirit.

I'm not religious, nor am I an atheist. I wouldn't even call myself agnostic. I think there is wisdom to be had in organized efforts toward holiness, but I know there is also wickedness. So I believe in all the *good* in every religion. Around my neck I wear a chain adorned with a Star of David, a *hamsa,* a Russian Orthodox protection ring, and more that symbolize good and also hold my "powers." I'll take whatever blessings I can get.

Despite my far-reaching dabbling in the ways of God, I had never experienced anything like I did during this ceremony. I could feel everyone standing behind me, trying to push me up. It was a stunning array of love. The priest sweated with emotion as he made me strong for competition and confrontation.

In the last and most glorious preparation for the Olympics, I relieved my soul of all the trials I had gone through in the last four years. I was now ready to head into battle.

Galina popped out of the overloaded van at the Olympic Village in Vancouver wearing a pair of heels and a long mink dyed the color of merlot. I followed her in knee-high, pointy-toed boots and a big, black, furry jacket that screamed *ta-da!* One of the helpers deposited our luggage (we each had something like six pieces) and then sped off to another area.

Passing us on all sides were Russians in their Bosco Sport uniforms, Americans decked head to toe in red, white, and blue, and Italians in sleek Lycra courtesy of Mr. Armani. Literally every single person ran around, all day, every day, wearing a patriotically inspired athletic ensemble. Even their underwear had flags on it.

With everyone in sneakers and sweats, they stared at us in our fanciest (and perhaps most ridiculous) getups and most likely thought, *Whose team are they on?*

Answer: we weren't part of any team. Not really.

Despite all the usual stress and strain of an Olympic season, Galina and I managed to maintain a great relationship and spent the entire games on the same wavelength, which was completely independent. We didn't feel a part of the Americans because of all the bad blood, and yet we couldn't get too cozy with the Russians for political reasons. So it was always just the two of us—decked in our finest amid a sea of sportsmen.

During team processing, Galina, in Russian, mocked the American team uniforms, saying that they looked like an exact replica of the jackets worn by construction workers in Moscow. Adding to the improbability that any of those clothes would touch my body, there were no uniforms available in my size. Instead, one of the officials handed me a jacket and pants with Day-Glo detailing in size extra-large, which sent Galina off on a stream of untranslatable and unprintable insults. She didn't like the uniforms but wanted to be the one to reject them.

After the team processing meetings, we went to find our accommodations. Newly built, million-dollar condos right on the water that had yet to hit Vancouver's real estate market housed members of the Olympic teams during our stay. In the building reserved for the American team, Galina and I headed up to the sixth floor, and as soon as we stepped off the elevator almost had a heart attack. The walls looked like they were bleeding.

One American team leader from Kansas had decorated the entire hallway with hundreds of small plastic American flags and red-white-and-blue streamers. It was very festive and rah-rah in a blinding sort of way.

Galina and I split up as one of the coordinators showed me down the dizzying hall and around the corner to my room. The door opened to a gigantic apartment with magnificent floor-to-ceiling windows that boasted a view of the harbor as well as the planetarium, which had been taken over and decorated for

Russia House. Huge signs saying "Sochi," the Russian city hosting the next winter Olympics, covered the domed building. I found the sight incredibly cheerful.

I grabbed the bigger bedroom because my roommate, Tanith Belbin, wasn't going to be arriving for a few days, and flopped down on the bed, letting my pointy boots hang off the end. Soaking in my palatial surroundings (way better than the five-women-to-two-bedroom ratio Galina faced down the hall), I felt empty.

My slightly depressed state was so different from that of my first Olympics, when I'd found myself bouncing off the walls with excitement. In the back of my mind a sobering thought loomed: my innocence was almost over. I would soon have to grow up and become a real person whose life isn't planned out from morning to night. It was as foreboding as the harbor's black, choppy water that I stared at from my bed. This Olympics almost certainly marked the end of my competitive career. My entire identity, the thing that I had breathed almost every moment of my life since the age of thirteen, would suddenly change. And yet I had no idea what lay ahead. What would I do without skating?

That heaviness remained with me for the opening ceremonies. As I've said, when it comes to parties and anything where there's an enforced protocol, I'm not a big fan. And there's nothing more enforced than the Olympics' opening ceremony. The American team members had a very specific costume we had to wear (explained in detail on a printed handout), and if you didn't follow it, you couldn't walk. While wearing the sweater, hat, pin, and other mandatory garb, I tried my best to make myself look like I wasn't part of the masses as I gave my cheekbones extra definition and let my hair peek out from under the hat.

Even though Vancouver hosted the first indoor opening ceremonies for the Winter Olympics, all the athletes still wore sweaters, parkas, hats, and boots. It was the winter games, after all, and we had to look the part. But with balmy outdoor temperatures in the forties and fifties, it became excruciatingly hot with thousands of bundled-up bodies waiting in a concrete sweat lodge beneath the stadium. It got pretty disgusting.

When they released us from burning up in the pen into a winter wonderland with fake snow raining down inside the stadium, I walked the whole lap, trying to soak up the spirit from the crowd screaming with enthusiasm. Once I finished the lap, I told a helper from the organizing committee: "Okay, I'm ready."

Back in my room, I took a bubble bath to clean myself up from my sweaty mess. Relaxed after a nice long soak, I walked out onto the balcony, which afforded a bird's-eye view of the stadium and the opening ceremonies still going on. Sitting for a while alone, I could hear the roar of the crowd and see the ending display of fireworks that looked from a distance like nothing more than a child's sparkler. When the cold began to penetrate my clothes, I went back inside and spent the rest of the night doing laundry.

———————

The day of the short program, I felt so confident and so good it was bizarre. I had slept well and even taken a nap comfortably—shocking for a bad sleeper like me. But Canada is good for sleeping. I didn't get sweaty palms doing my hair and makeup. I was so prepared for battle that nothing could affect me, not even the debacle of my practice the day before.

I was the only one of the three American men who chose to do the late-night practice, which was published in the official schedule for everyone to see. The practices, like everything else at the Olympics, are an extremely formal affair because it's required for at least one official and one doctor to attend whenever an athlete is on the ice.

But when Galina and I got to the rink that night, we were the only ones there. After a few minutes I turned to Galina and said, "Nobody's here."

It was a shocking oversight in a place where, for random drug-testing purposes, athletes can't even leave a building without alerting an official.

"Well, Johnny, you knew coming into this we'd be alone," she said.

I did know that, but it had never been so in my face. The night before one of the biggest performances of my life, my country couldn't even show me the respect of coming to my last practice. I had done my part, giving great practices, interviews, and the publicity they wanted for the team. Still, they couldn't even do the basics of their job when it came to me.

As a sign of respect, I had worn to practice one of the jackets from the team processing—although, in keeping with my vow after the Nationals, this one didn't say "USA." But I immediately took it off and threw it on the other side of the boards. I was my own team, representing my fans and my country but not the federation.

Galina told me to get on the ice. "Our doctor's here," she said, pointing to the Russian doctor standing right behind her. Two Russian officials, who had come for Evgeni Plushenko's practice before mine, kindly stayed to monitor me.

The next day at the competition I thanked them again for their help, choosing not to engage in any way with my own team officials who made no excuses for their absence at my practice. Yes, the Olympics could be a little like high school.

Alas, the ridiculousness wasn't over. As we warmed up, the organizing committee had decided to air mini bios of each skater, flashing portraits of us on a jumbo screen and broadcasting thumbnail sketches of our lives through the stadium. As part of the second to last group, I skated with five other big contenders. Everyone's string of credits—like Brian Joubert's titles that included world champion and two-time European champion—sounded formidable over the booming loudspeaker.

And then came mine. I got on the ice and as my picture popped up, the announcer read: "Johnny Weir from the United States of America. Johnny speaks French and Russian. He has a TV show and enjoys fashion." I couldn't believe my ears. *Why do I have that?*

While everyone else had their hometown and skating credentials, my description sounded like a fucked-up singles ad. *Johnny loves Bordeaux and long walks on the beach.* No mention that I was the three-time United States national champion, world bronze medalist, or Grand Prix final bronze medalist. Nope, my whole life of dedicating myself to this sport boiled down to this fact: "Oh, he likes fashion."

Galina was laughing when I got off the ice, and I'm pretty sure a lot of other people were, too. But nothing could shake me. I was ready to literally show my life's work to the world.

I took my starting position for my program, which I had titled *I Love You, I Hate You,* a fairly accurate description of my relationship to the skating world. The music by Raul Di Blasio started out slowly in a reflection of my classical side, and feeling the beauty of the melody, I nailed my first three jumps. After I went into a spin, the music flipped into a dirty rumba, where I could showcase a spicier side. I wiggled my butt and started giving major face, flying through the steps and actually having fun. I flirted with the audience and the judges, and before I knew it, the whole thing was over.

After months and months of single-minded determination in the lead-up to the Olympics, my first moment on the ice was over, and it had been perfect. My astonishment gave way to excitement and a tremendous sense of accomplishment. Even Galina was happy. "Poker Face" came on the loudspeakers as I moved to the kiss and cry, and I danced in my seat to my celebratory anthem.

Then my scores came up and they were anything but a celebration. I had placed a shocking fifth, and there were still six more skaters after me. That meant I could wind up in a stomach-churning eleventh place. What had I done? What was wrong? I thought my skating had been podium worthy, and there were only a few times in my career where my perceptions and scores had not matched up. Galina, sensing my quickly surfacing outrage, said between smiling teeth for the camera: "Of course they did this to you. Don't be shocked. Just deal with it. The people love you and respect you."

The audience started booing and whistling. It was an incredibly harsh moment on the heels of such a feeling of triumph. While the fans may have loved and supported me, those in charge of the medals, and pretty much my value as an athlete, weren't buying it.

I ended up in sixth place after everyone competed in the short program. But it could have been a lot worse. Despite my poor placement, I still had a fighting chance for a medal. The pressure was on. In the long program, I would be the second to last skater in the entire competition, the opening act to Plushenko's finale.

But my scores were so low, I was barely ahead of people that had made mistakes and nearly fallen. It was a depressing hole to dig out of from a competitor's perspective.

I wasn't happy. What Olympic athlete, even one as weird as me, doesn't want to win a medal? Going into the long program, however, my main objective was no longer winning. How could it be? Instead, I wanted to take everyone watching me—in the building, on the judges' panel, on TV at home—on a journey. I wanted to make them all cry, or at least feel something. Making people cry was the goal of my free program from the beginning and the first way I described what I wanted to do to Galina.

The journey was my own. I had conceived of my long program, entitled *Fallen Angel,* as my life story on the ice. Throughout my career, there were high moments when everyone loved me, but the minute I fell, I plummeted to the lowest depths of hell. Soaring or broken, spinning or still, this was me for everyone to see.

Right before I took the ice for my final Olympic competition, I certainly had enough emotion in me to share with every member of the crowd. In quite possibly my last moment in the spotlight, the stress and passion of the last thirteen years turned into pure energy; my life flashing before me faster than a boy on skates.

"You can do this," Galina said. "You're the prettiest, the smartest, the strongest. Just let yourself do this."

Then there was just ice and the lights, and nothing else mattered.

Every arena is very bright and has its own special aura. But in Vancouver it was as if I were skating in a bubble of light. Like a moth to a flame, the light, which I normally shunned, drew me in and made me feel gorgeous.

Angelic voices sent me off on my final journey. The movements that I had honed in countless hours on the ice, and in countless more of deprivation off of it, carried me through the steps. Artistry took me to the end. Every person in that arena held his breath until the music and I stopped in a big flourish. As I lay upside down in a backbend, the ice became the sky, my trapped version of heaven.

I remained on my knees for a few moments, forever the supplicant, but when I stood up, I saw people were also standing, as well as crying. I got exactly what I wanted. At that point it didn't matter what result came up. It didn't matter what place I got. It didn't matter who was ahead of me. In that moment I felt like I was the Champion, the only one.

The rest is history. I placed sixth overall to boos and cries of outrage, and Evan took home the gold, the first American to win the Olympic title since 1988.

In sports, you have to come up with your own concept of victory, because you won't always win. Yes, I wanted recognition in my sport through medals. It hurt when all the years I had spent falling, hurting, bleeding, and crying got chalked up to my liking fashion. In the last four years of my career, the problem of my appearing like a flake worsened. People never talked about my skating. Instead, they talked about the crazy things that I enjoyed or said. I'm colorful and entertaining, but that's not all I am. As an athlete, I'm extremely competitive.

But I was able to leave any bitterness behind for my last Olympic performance. For whatever reason—and I'm not a big believer in a personal god—I felt that God was with me and all I had done up to then was leading me to that very moment. Having been beaten down so many times, I proved one more time that I always rose back up.

So this was no longer a competition. At least not for me. Obviously, realizing you aren't going to win is a hard thing for an athlete to accept. But as a person you have to take the victories where you get them. And my victory was showing my face. The Olympic champion got to where he was because he worked very hard, as I did, and played by the rules, as I did not. People that win may not always win on their own terms. Looking out at the Olympic ice, I had the honor of having arrived there on my own terms.

After the public and private outcries, shock, and ultimately acceptance, I left the stadium, and a chapter of my life, returning to my room in the quiet of late night. Tanith was already sleeping, so I tiptoed through the apartment and went into the bathroom.

As I began wiping the makeup off my face, I had my first chance to really look at myself. The eyes looking back at me almost seemed like they belonged to a different person. When they started watering, I thought the makeup remover was the culprit. I tried wiping them with a tissue, but soon enough I realized these were tears of emotion.

All I wanted to do was scream to release whatever was growing inside me. But I couldn't because Tanith was sleeping. So I got into the big stone shower, and, sitting underneath the stream of very hot water, let myself yell and cry as loud as I wanted. I was in there for more than an hour because I couldn't stop the flow of aggression, frustration, and happiness that I had pent up as a warrior.

When I got out of the shower, I had seventy or eighty voice mails and hundreds of text messages, but I only answered one. "Thank you, Mom," I texted. "I love you. I'm going to bed."

Although I was still crying softly, I had to get on with it. So I moisturized, watched half an episode of *The Rachel Zoe Project*, took an Ambien, and passed out.

First thing the next morning, I went to the condo where my family was staying. Walking into the house, it felt like a funeral had just taken place. I hadn't seen my mother since before my Olympic moment, and she was the first one to grab me. She had dark circles under her eyes from exhaustion and immediately upon seeing me, her lip started to quiver. Neither of us could speak because of those familiar tears that began to well up. Finally my mom choked out a small, tight "I'm so proud of you."

I moved on to the rest of my family, all of whom were crestfallen. My dad, brother, aunts, grandmother, and cousins, none of them knew what to say to me. It was just like when somebody's died. They all wanted things to be different, for me to have walked away with any color of medal as a material symbol that the last thirteen years of my life, and all of our lives, had been a success.

We just sat there and talked about everything, except what had happened the night before. "Oh, we have this cake from

Whole Foods," one of my cousins offered. "It's really good if you heat it up in the microwave."

In the middle of this strained attempt at normal conversation, my mother blurted out, "Johnny, I am so fucking pissed."

Everyone else went silent.

"Mom, you don't even have to talk to me. I know. I'm with you."

To be honest, I wasn't pissed at that point. It did break my heart to see my family so devastated, but perhaps the hardest part was that we didn't have a "next thing" to talk about. I didn't have anything planned or to plan. Galina and I had talked about my going to the World Championships a month after the Olympics, and we had practice time booked a few days later to begin training. But inwardly I had pretty much decided that I wouldn't go. It would crush me to have two events in one month where I did my best and didn't get rewarded for it. I didn't want to risk that kind of defeat.

For the duration of my time in Vancouver, I found it far easier to deal with the media than my family—a good thing since Tara had me booked for days from morning until night. The constant whirlwind of going from gigs to interviews, giving everyone my best Johnny flair, kept any kind of existential crisis at bay.

In the middle of the madness, Dorothy Hamill was set to interview me for *Access Hollywood,* but before filming started she said, "I have something delicate I want to talk to you about. Tell me if it's okay."

Two broadcasters from Quebec had said on air that I needed a gender test, because they didn't know if I was a man or a woman. They also complained that I set a "bad example" for boys who want to skate because parents feared they'd end up like me. Apparently they felt that my costume and body language made me a degenerate.

"Yeah, of course, it's fine," I told Dorothy. I didn't really think anything of it because it was just two assholes speaking in French on a small network in Quebec.

Boy, was I wrong. A whole new round of interview requests came in. Everyone wanted me to respond to these random guys calling me a woman—not exactly an insult in my book. I could have talked about it for hours; what did I care? But Tara didn't like my freewheeling style and had me hold a press conference to address the randoms in a more dignified and official manner.

Ten days after I had placed sixth, when I should have been a total irrelevance at the Olympic games, I walked into a room crowded with reporters looking for me to talk about two Quebecois frat boys. Okay, if that's what the people wanted, I was more than happy to oblige.

The funny thing is that I wasn't offended. I made it clear in the press conference that I hoped these guys didn't get fired, because I believe in freedom of speech and freedom of opinion. But I refuted the notion that I set anything but a great example for kids.

I'm not ashamed to be me. On the contrary, I think I turned

out pretty great and am proud of my individuality. I mostly had my parents and the caring and free way they raised me to thank. More than anyone else I know, I love my life and accept myself. What's wrong with being unique?

My speaking out was not just for the gay world, not at all. At the Olympics, I had received bucketloads of hand-drawn cards from kids, and I thought if there is one out there like me, but who doesn't have a supportive family or friends, then I owe it to him. So it was for gay kids, but also the kids who like science even if it's not cool, or kids who like to stand like a flamingo with one leg tucked up underneath for hours, as I did as a child. My message was for all the "weirdos" of the world.

I'm not sure I would have held a press conference like that before my experience at the Olympics where I fully realized the beauty and power in making a connection with others. Despite my heartbreaking loss, I was made whole again by having people say to me in letters or on the streets of the Olympic Village, "We went on this journey with you. We felt you." As clichéd as it sounds, their sentiment was worth its weight in gold.

My entire life came down to those ten minutes that I spent in front of the world in February of 2010. Whether alone, in front of a single person, or, like me, millions, everyone experiences an instant when one's essence is brought forth in a single act of bravery. To the universe, you say: this is who I am. In my performance I revealed my guts, my gusto, my heart, everything that I am. I showed my soul. Because of that, it was and will always be the moment of my life.

Epilogue

The ice is frozen, like always. The rink is cold and familiar. I am bundled in one too many sweatshirts, the outermost one with "Russia" embroidered across the back. Staring at a dozen children, all under ten years old, flying around the ice with a look that's a mixture of bliss, concentration, and a little bit of terror, I can't help but wonder what will become of them. What kind of people will they grow into? Will they have happy lives? Will any of them become an Olympic star? One of the children soars into the air to practice her single axel, crashing to the ice with an indignant thud.

Watching the girl brings me back to the first time I did an

axel. Only fourteen years have passed since my first foray onto the ice in the group of Orange Circles. Only fourteen years since I'd shed tears from the blistering cold of flying around on ice outdoors in the dead of winter. Only fourteen years since I'd turned my entire family's life upside down financially and emotionally for a dream. Only fourteen years to go from a nothing in a nothing town to a two-time Olympian and artist.

Even though it has been months since my greatest artistic breakthrough at the Olympics in Vancouver, I am still as regimented and tight-assed about my life as always. Old habits die hard. Because my public life is such a constant peacock display of insanity, my life behind the scenes needs to be as strict as a communist regime. I wake up early once a week and do everything I can possibly do to make my home a spotless oasis of serenity and glamour, including vacuuming my carpet and freshly mopping and Swiffering my wood floors. All the dishes are washed (the Fabergé crystal goblets by hand). The cupboards are fully stocked with only the best things Whole Foods has to offer. I do laundry and catch up on dry cleaning. The Louboutins are freshly polished. The photos and tchotchkes are shining with a new coat of Windex.

Everything is absolutely precise, a trait I learned from my father. Dinner happens before five p.m. Bedtime is promptly at ten p.m. And skating still takes precedence over all other activities.

My life at home is so concrete because a job pushed aside never gets done—and the only person who knows how to do the job correctly is me. So despite jet lag, preparing for a skating show, personal appearances, recording a song, or raising my family of Dingles (aka my closest group of friends), I never stray from a level of compulsion that most would find terrifying.

That side of me seems so opposite to my public persona—overly flamboyant, wildly optimistic, incredibly sparkly, and Liza with a z—that one could accuse me of being bipolar. But isn't every true artist a little crazy?

I only let colorful Johnny out on special occasions, like my recent twenty-sixth birthday.

To prepare for the big bash, my makeup professional, Joey from MAC, met me at Tara's Manhattan apartment to unleash my inner lady with a lot of product. Tara—who started using a cleaning lady because I can't prepare for anything in chaos and I'm in her apartment almost daily for one reason or another—applied her own fake lashes in her spotless bathroom.

As bottles of champagne chilled in the fridge, a hundred balloons wrapped in a giant plastic condom were delivered to me and released in the apartment. Joey fluttered his wrist in a final application of bronzer.

"Girl, you're gorgeous," he said, admiring his work.

"Thank you, Josephina!"

Tara trotted into the living room on five-inch stilettos, which made me proud.

"Are you ready?" she asked.

"I was born ready."

Twenty minutes later all the Dingles and other friends

started pouring into the apartment. Tara's boyfriend Marshmallow arrived followed by a slew of Russians. Paris came fashionably late with NicoFierce, just before my costume designer swooped in for a birthday eve hug. After lots of champagne toasts, the billion people, crowded into Tara's small place, crowded into a Hummer limo and headed to da club.

When I got out of the giant luxury car, I was greeted by a swarm of paparazzi and a club manager, who warned me "*Page Six* is here" and undoubtedly tipped them off. They were in good company. Inside, so many people had gathered to wish me well: famous fashion designers Chris Benz and Richie Rich, New York socialites, The Beauty Bears Eric and Joey. It seemed everyone had a "+7" next to their names on the list. *Come one, come all.* I don't party often, but when I'm in charge of the party, everyone is invited.

I fluttered around pouring champagne and chatting with everyone just like any mother would do. Out of the corner of my eye, I saw boys kissing boys, ladies grinding with drag queens, men having heart to hearts (I prefer soul to soul). Among the inexplicable fashions and inspired dancing, I stood alone next to a banquette, and in a quiet, shocking moment realized the fogged-up atrium was filled with people I loved. Each, in some way, represented a small piece of my soul, who I am deep down. The colorful, the demure, the bold, the clever. I looked closely at my family and friends for an image of myself, as they are my mirror.

Back in the rink, watching the child fall on her axel attempt, I'm faced with another kind of mirror. *Life is gonna knock you down a lot, honey.* I think to myself of all the times I've been knocked down. The betrayals of childhood friends, the numerous dips in my career, falling on quad attempt after quad attempt, being judged for things I had no control over, starving myself for the sake of art, and the list goes on and on. The common denominator of all those moments was the ferocity with which I forced myself to claw my way back up and move ahead. Fail on your first try at the Olympics? Go again and prove you aren't a quitter and you are tough as nails. Give the people in your life someone to be proud of but, most important, make yourself proud. Love yourself.

Love myself I do. Not everything, but I love the good as well as the bad. I love my crazy lifestyle, and I love my hard discipline. I love my freedom of speech and the way my eyes get dark when I'm tired. I love that I have learned to trust people with my heart, even if it will get broken. I am proud of everything that I am and will become. I am proud to have the honor of being born with the last name Weir (no matter our bad luck, it is my father's name). I love that I am my mother's son, and that she is my confidante and main inspiration in life. I love that I am a big brother to the gentlest soul yet the toughest exterior that is Boz. Yes, I love myself, and every time I fall down, especially when I fall down, I find that love again.

"JOHNNYCHIK! JOHNIK! CHEBURASHKA U NAS (OUR CHEBURASHKA)*!* GET BACK TO WORK! *DAVAI!"*

Like a voice from across Siberia, the sound snaps me out of my reverie. Distinct and knowing, rich and cultured, terrifying and loving, it's Galina Yakovlevna Zmievskaya cajoling me to continue skating. I glide away from the small girl who's now skating into another axel jump with that familiar look of anticipation that says, *Will I succeed or fail?*

A small smile breaks my porcelain exterior as I remember a young boy running across his backyard in a pair of hand-me-down ice skates, arms flailing wildly as he slides onto a frozen cornfield in the middle of nowhere, wrapped in snowsuits lovingly applied by his mother and, in his mind, imagining himself on the world's biggest stage, full of pride, honor, and love.

Acknowledgments

The list of people who I need to thank seems impossibly long and thanking them is simply not enough. I have undying gratitude and love for all of you, and I hope we can all continue to make each other proud and strong simply by being.

First and foremost I need to thank my legions of fans around the world. I would never be who I am without you. Johnny's Angels were the first real group to take shape, and I have been so honored to go on my journey through life with you and with your full support. Your group begat so many others: weir.ru in Russia, Johnny's Japanese Angels in Japan, and many others from China to Ukraine, France to South America. You all really are angels, in every sense of that word, and I am forever in your debt.

My family has been my greatest inspiration and support system since I came into this world, and they have never wavered in their love for me despite how difficult I can make it for them. My grandparents, Marcella and Robert "Puff" Moore and Faye and John Weir; my aunts Diane, Cindy, Terry, and Deborah; my uncles Joel and Bobby; my cousins Joel, Audra, Timothy, Stacey, and Shannon; and most of all my parents, John and Patti Weir, and my little brother, Boz. We have a giant extended family—and I wish they would give me extra pages to thank all of you by name—but you all know I love you and am thinking of you. You are all the light of my life.

My coaches and choreographers have given me the gift of sport and taught me about the world outside my small town upbringing and given me the freedom I so desperately crave: Priscilla Hill, Galina Zmievskaya, Nina Petrenko, Viktor Petrenko, Tatiana Tarasova, Marina Anissina, David Wilson, Elena Tchaikovskaya, Yuri Sergeev, Denis Petukhov, Melissa Gregory and Faye Kitariev. Thank you for helping me show the world what I am made of.

I would go absolutely nowhere without my amazing agent and resident Jewish sister, Tara Modlin. I often say that I am a rhino, and Tara is the little bird sitting on my shoulder and telling me about danger and triumph, and that analogy couldn't be truer. I want to also thank Tara's family and especially Grandma Connie, who is the original reason we got together. I love you, Taryuha!

I am possibly one of the most difficult friends to have, but my friends make up my inner circle, my confidants, the true loves of my life: Paris Childers, Christa Goulakos, Nicole Haddad, Michael Dudas, Christopher Gale, Jodi Rudden, Kelly Bailey, Dirke Baker, Bradford Griffies, Drew Meekins, Kendra Goodwin, Tanith Belbin, Irina Slutskaya, Evgeni Plushenko, Marina Anissina, Alexander Uspenski, Rudy Galindo, Sasha and Roman Zaretsky, Ksenia Makarova, Michela Malingambi, and many, many more of you who I love to no end.

Thank you to figure skating, and those who created a platform for me to perform, and inspire myself. Thank you to David Raith and Patricia St. Peter for being two angels among many devils. Thank you to the skaters, past, present, and future for giving us beauty and showing us what a real sport is.

I absolutely need to thank everyone who helped me on this project, otherwise it never would have gotten to the point where people could actually read it! Everyone at Gallery Books and Simon & Schuster; Patrick Price, my amazing editor; Jen Bergstrom for getting this project off the ground; Mitchell Ivers and Jessica Webb for shepherding the work in house. Thank you to Dan Strone, CEO of Trident Media Group, my amazing literary agent, who believed in me so much, and his assistant Lyuba Di-Falco; and Rebecca "Lucky" Paley, my muse for this entire project, never wavering in her support or love for me, and, although neither of us "play well with others," became such a close friend and confidante. Thank you for believing in me.

It doesn't seem fitting to "thank" the people who have made

my life difficult or who have given me a fight every step of the way, but I salute everyone who has ever criticized me, not believed in me, or belittled me, for you are the ones who have given me a thick skin and made it possible for me to fight for everything I believe in and fight for those I love. You also have given me the will to succeed in every facet of my life.

I need to thank the visionaries and divas of the world for dancing to your own tunes and making it possible for the younger generations to have hope and strength to be unique. I gained strength from people like Elton John, Christina Aguilera, Lady Gaga, Ricky Martin, Alexander Pushkin, Rudolf Nureyev, Mikhail Baryshnikov, Edith Piaf, Karl Lagerfeld, and many more; and for your unknown contributions to my life I thank you.

A mother's love is what sustains us as humans, and I have the best possible image of what a mother would, should, and could be. Patti Ann Moore Weir is my mother, my best friend, and my constant cheerleader. She has been the greatest inspiration in my life, and will be that for me until my last breath. There are no words grand enough to thank her with. I love you, Mama.